SELECTED POEMS
OF
THOMAS MERTON

By Thomas Merton

THE ASIAN JOURNAL
CABLES TO THE ACE
THE COLLECTED POEMS
GANDHI ON NON-VIOLENCE
THE GEOGRAPHY OF LOGRAIRE
MY ARGUMENT WITH THE GESTAPO
NEW SEEDS OF CONTEMPLATION
RAIDS ON THE UNSPEAKABLE
SELECTED POEMS
THE STRANGE ISLANDS
THE WAY OF CHUANG TZU
THE WISDOM OF THE DESERT
ZEN AND THE BIRDS OF APPETITE

Published by
New Directions

SELECTED POEMS

OF

THOMAS MERTON

WITH AN INTRODUCTION BY

MARK VAN DOREN

ENLARGED EDITION

A NEW DIRECTIONS PAPERBOOK

Library of Congress Catalog Card No. 67-23488

(ISBN: 0-8112-0100-7)

First Published in 1959

Enlarged edition, 1967

Manufactured in the United States of America

Published in Canada by George J. McLoed Ltd., Toronto

New Directions Books are published for James Laughlin
by New Directions Publishing Corporation,
80 Eighth Avenue, New York 10011

NINTH PRINTING

CONTENTS

INTRODUCTION

by

Mark Van Doren

INTRODUCTION

In the summer of 1953 Thomas Merton wrote to me from Gethsemani: "Our cow barn burned down in little over twenty minutes or half an hour—like a pile of brush. We could do nothing to put it out. Everybody thought it was a really beautiful fire, and it was. I am sending you a poem about it." The poem was "Elegy for the Monastery Barn," and I liked it so much that six years later, when I knew I was going to write this preface, I wrote Merton saying I hoped it would be among the poems he had selected. He replied: "I forget whether or not I included the Barn on the original list, perhaps I was shy about it. As a matter of fact it is for me subjectively an important poem, because when I was a kid on a farm in Maryland (yes, even that, for a while) a barn burned down in the middle of the night and it is one of the earliest things I can remember. So burning barns are for me great mysteries that are important. They turn out to be the whole world, and it is the Last Judgement."

Well, the poem is here, and it is as good a place as any to start looking at and listening to the poet in Thomas Merton. But one further document has a bearing on the subject. The preface to *The Strange Islands,* 1957, ends with these sentences: " 'Elegy for the Monastery Barn' was written after the cowbarn at Gethsemani burned down, one August evening in 1953, during the evening meditation. The monks left the meditation to fight a very hot fire and the poem arrived about the same time as the fire truck from the nearest town." The bearing is in the humor, which Merton never is without, and in the knowledge he keeps of the way things go in this world. The slowness of the truck, the swiftness of the poem, the childhood memory: all of these are somehow there, illuminating if not explaining the happy power awakened in Merton's mind as it races through the realities of his theme. For the burning barn is really an old lady dressed for her last hour in unaccountable finery, nor is any distinction to be made between her proud cries and the crackling of the flames. And she leaves us when she is gone with delicate memories of what she had been during the years when we ignored her: of her solitude, her peace, her patience as she waited for this end. The fifty invisible cattle, the fifty past years, are just as real; and so at the close is Merton's flight into another dimension where the Holy One sits in the presence of disaster. All is real; nothing is made up; this, we instantly believe, is the true content of the subject, which like any other subject starts on earth and gets in its own natural way to heaven.

Such, I take it, is what Merton means in the note on "Poetry and Contemplation," which appeared in an earlier edition. He says there, better he thinks than he did ten years ago, and in this I believe him to be right, that poetry at its best *is* contemplation—of things, and of what they signify. Not what they can be made to signify, but what they actually do signify, even when nobody knows it. The better the poet, the more we are convinced that he has knowledge of this kind, and has it humbly. "The earliest fathers," Merton wrote me in 1954, "knew that all things, as such, are symbolic by their very being and nature, and all talk of something beyond themselves. Their meaning is not something we impose upon them, but a mystery which we can discover in them, if we have the eyes to look with." The right eyes for the purpose are keen and honest, and there had better be some humor in them too. At least that is where poetry begins, whether its aim is religious or not. And certainly, if its aim is religious, it must begin there if it is ever to move us deeply. Religious poetry is rooted in things as much as any other kind of poetry is. Without that root it is merely pious, as its secular counterpart is merely poetical.

The sight and sound and feel of things is everywhere in Merton's poetry. Consider the first line of "Trappists, Working":

Now all our saws sing holy sonnets in this
    world of timber.

The sound, so sudden and robust, brings with it a sense of the joy with which it is made, and the context of that joy. Perhaps there is no sound at all in the beginning lines of "The Trappist Cemetery—Gethsemani":

Brothers, the curving grasses and their daughters
Will never print your praises.

But no sound was intended; the prim alliteration in the second line is like a finger laid upon the lips, forbidding speech where no speech would be proper. The silence asked for here is nothing like the heavier sort that states itself in the first of "Three Postcards from the Monastery":

> The pilgrim passes swiftly.
> All the strange towns,
> Wrapped in their double cloaks
> (Of rain and of non-entity)
> Veil their elusive faces.

The wit of the parenthesis is no less deadly for being all but voiceless, as befits the faceless towns behind their veils of rain. What a plenitude of sound, however, comes to us out of eleven words in "The Trappist Abbey: Matins,"

> where some train runs, lost,
> Baying in eastward mysteries of distance.

And again it is true that the thing we hear speaks of more than itself; its skilful music is in the service of a thought so wide that all the world at dawn, near by and far away, is sleepily included. Elsewhere we read:

> But sound is never half so fair
> As when that music turns to air
> And the universe dies of excellence.

Those lines from "A Psalm" bring sound to a dead stop, drowned as it were in itself, and signifying by its very extinction the universe beyond sense.

Sight and sound and feeling. I have spoken so far only of sound, and indeed that may be enough, for in

the poetry of Thomas Merton all the senses work to-
gether to one end, the letting of things declare them-
selves. Which of the senses is dominant, for instance,
in this passage from "The Sowing of Meanings"?

For, like a grain of fire
Smouldering in the heart of every living essence
God plants His undivided power—
Buries His thought too vast for worlds
In seed and root and blade and flower,
Until, in the amazing light of April,
Surcharging the religious silence of the spring,
Creation finds the pressure of his everlasting
     secret
Too terrible to bear.
Then everywhere we look, lo! rocks and trees
Pastures and hills and streams and birds and
     firmament
And our own souls within us flash.

It is something to be seen and heard and felt in one
miraculous moment; also, to be wondered at and
contemplated, thought about and blissfully forgot-
ten. Yet sound is somehow for Merton the carrying
sense, the medium through which experience of any
magnitude makes itself seen and felt. Of any magni-
tude—a reminder that Merton is a noticer of little
things as well as huge ones. Of children, for instance,
and their

     little voices, light as stems of lilies.

Are these voices heard or seen? Or felt? It does not matter, in view of the unearthly sweetness they signify, any more than it matters how we decide to explain the magic by which St. Agnes, with no thought of us in her small head, steals all our love as we behold her.

> Hear with what joy this child of God
> Plays in the perfect garden of her
>   martyrdom, . . .
> Spending the silver of her little life
> To bring her Bridegroom these bright flowers
> Of which her arms are full. . . .
> Her virtues, with their simple strings,
> Play to the Lover hidden in the universe.

The foregoing would suggest that the special reputation of Merton's poem "For My Brother: Reported Missing in Action, 1943" is not an accident. No poem in the book is better known, and the reason may lie in the music it makes. It is the kind of music that only poetry can make: not pure sound, of course, but something buried in the words and (in this case) mourning there. *The Seven-Storey Mountain* tells the story of the brother's death in prose that moves the reader too; without, however, assembling the sounds that are climaxed here in two paradoxical verses:

> The silence of Whose tears shall fall
> Like bells upon your alien tomb.

The poem, having created its own silence in preparation for these lines, drops them into our imagination where it is possible for tears that make no noise to sound nevertheless like delicate, distinct bronze, hopelessly far away. The figures of the poem are justly celebrated: the sleepless eyes as flowers, the fasts as willows, the thirst as springs, and the money of breath and death and weeping. Yet figures alone do not make a great poem. There must be a music that absorbs them and relates them, and gives them in the end a power for which we cannot assign the cause. We can say that the very intensity of the poet's fear that he will fail is somehow the reason for his success; we can guess that inarticulate grief manages here, simply because it must, to become articulate after all; but it is truer to say that in such a poem sadness sings—a low note, in perfect pitch, that carries around the world.

For Merton there is another world beyond this one where his brother died, and where he himself writes poetry. But the poetry is a way to that world. Indeed, given his endowment, is may well be *the* way, so that mystic and poet, seer and singer, in his case are one.

MARK VAN DOREN

SELECTED POEMS
OF
THOMAS MERTON

LENT IN A YEAR OF WAR

One of you is a major, made of cord and catskin,

But never dreams his eyes may come to life and thread
The needle-light of famine in a waterglass.

One of you is the paper Jack of Sprites
And will not cast his sentinel voice
Spiraling up the dark ears of the wind
Where the prisoner's yell is lost.

> "What if it was our thumbs put out the sun
> When the Lance and Cross made their mistake?
> You'll never rob us our Eden of drumskin shel-
>   ters,
> You, with the bite of John the Baptist's halter,
> Getting away in the basket of Paul,
> Loving the answer of death, the mother of Lent!"

Thus, in the evening of their sinless murders,
Jack and the Major, sifting the stars for a sign
See the north-south horizon parting like a string!

3

THE FLIGHT INTO EGYPT

Through every precinct of the wintry city
Squadroned iron resounds upon the streets;
Herod's police
Make shudder the dark steps of the tenements
At the business about to be done.

Neither look back upon Thy starry country,
Nor hear what rumors crowd across the dark
Where blood runs down those holy walls,
Nor frame a childish blessing with Thy hand
Towards that fiery spiral of exulting souls!

Go, Child of God, upon the singing desert,
Where, with eyes of flame,
The roaming lion keeps thy road from harm.

SONG FOR OUR LADY OF COBRE

The white girls lift their heads like trees,
The black girls go
Reflected like flamingoes in the street.

The white girls sing as shrill as water,
The black girls talk as quiet as clay.

4

The white girls open their arms like clouds,
The black girls close their eyes like wings:
Angels bow down like bells,
Angels look up like toys,

Because the heavenly stars
Stand in a ring:
And all the pieces of the mosaic, earth,
Get up and fly away like birds.

THE NIGHT TRAIN

In the unreason of a rainy midnight
France blooms along the windows
Of my sleepy bathysphere,
And runs to seed in a luxuriance of curious lights.

Escape is drawn straight through my dream
And shines to Paris, clean as a violin string,
While spring tides of commotion,
(The third-class pianos of the Orient Express)
Fill the hollow barrels of my ears.

Cities that stood, by day, as gay as lancers
Are lost, in the night, like old men dying.
At a point where polished rails branch off forever
The steels lament, like crazy ladies.

We wake, and weep the deaths of the cathedrals
That we have never seen,
Because we hear the jugulars of the country
Fly in the wind, and vanish with a cry.

At once the diplomats start up, as white as bread,
Buckle the careless cases of their minds
That just fell open in the sleeper:

For, by the rockets of imaginary sieges
They see to read big, terrible print,
Each in the other's face,

That spells the undecoded names
Of the assassins they will recognise too late:
The ones that seem to be secret police,
Now all in place, all armed, in the obvious ambush.

SAINT JASON

This is the night the false Saint Jason
Wakes in fear from his cannibal sleep,
And drenches the edges of his eyes
With his tears' iron overflow;

For the flying scream of his dead woman
Opened the stitches of his skin,
And Jason bounced in the burly wind
Like a man of sack and string.

6

"What do you want, in the windows of your wound
Where Judas' money shines
By daggers' waterlight?"

"—I want the martyrs' eyes, as tight as shells,
In death's pretended sleep."

"What does it mean sunlight weeps in your door
Like an abandoned child?"

"—It means the heavyhanded storm,
Whirling and ploughing the wet woods,
Has filled with terrible speech
The stone doors of my feast:

The feast of the false Saint Jason's first communion."

THE MESSENGER

There is some sentry at the rim of winter
Fed with the speech the wind makes
In the grand belfries of the sleepless timber.

He understands the lasting strife of tears,
And the way the world is strung;
He waits to warn all life with the tongue of March's
    bugle,
Of the coming of the warrior sun.

When spring has garrisonned up her army of water,
A million grasses leave their tents, and stand in rows
To see their invincible brother.
Mending the winter's ruins with their laughter,
The flowers go out to their undestructive wars.

Walk in the woods and be witnesses,
You, the best of these poor children.

When Gabriel hit the bright shore of the world,
Yours were the eyes saw some
Star-sandalled stranger walk like lightning down the
      air,
The morning the Mother of God
Loved and dreaded the message of an angel.

THE REGRET

When cold November sits among the reeds like an un-
      lucky fisher

And ducks drum up as sudden as the wind
Out of the rushy river,
We slowly come, robbed of our rod and gun,
Walking amid the stricken cages of the trees.

The stormy weeks have all gone home like drunken
      hunters,
Leaving the gates of the grey world wide open to De-
      cember.

8

But now there is no speech of branches in these broken
    jails.
Acorns lie over the earth, no less neglected
Than our unrecognizable regret:
And here we stand as senseless as the oaks,
As dumb as elms.

And though we seem as grave as jailers, yet we did
    not come to wonder
Who picked the locks of the past days, and stole our
    summer.
(We are no longer listeners for curious saws, and
    secret keys!)

We are indifferent to seasons,
And stand like hills, deaf.
And never hear the last of the escaping year
Go ducking through the bended branches like a leaf.

AUBADE: LAKE ERIE

When sun, light handed, sows this Indian water
With a crop of cockles,
The vines arrange their tender shadows
In the sweet leafage of an artificial France.

Awake, in the frames of windows, innocent children,
Loving the blue, sprayed leaves of childish life,
Applaud the bearded corn, the bleeding grape,
And cry:

"Here is the hay-colored sun, our marvelous cousin,
Walking in the barley,
Turning the harrowed earth to growing bread,
And splicing the sweet, wounded vine.

Lift up your hitch-hiking heads
And no more fear the fever,
You fugitives, and sleepers in the fields,
Here is the hay-colored sun!"

And when their shining voices, clean as summer,
Play, like churchbells over the field,
A hundred dusty Luthers rise from the dead, un-
    heeding,
Search the horizon for the gap-toothed grin of fac-
    tories,
And grope, in the green wheat,
Toward the wood winds of the western freight.

POEM

Watching, among the rifled branches, for the sun, our
        hero,
(Sing, wind, too tuneless in the slender trees)

We think about a whiter day, the marble temples
And the hills, our girls,

The even lovelier skies,
The horses of Poseidon, the lifting seas,
All grave, and clean, and wiser than the glassy morn-
        ings.

Watching, among the colored rocks, the sea, our happy
        swimmer,
(Sing, winds, more clearly on the Greek acropoli)

We think about the cries of drowners and the shine of
        armor,
While the hills, our citadels,
The strict, immovable trees,
    (More marble than the marching winner
    Who winters in our corridors of discontent)
Grow cloudy, in the teeth of the command.

Waiting, among the rifled temples for the light, our
        savior,
(Play, winds, in this too voiceless choir of columns)

We think about the whiter colonnades, the wiser city,
While the green hills, our shambles,
The burning olive gardens,
Have made the country blinder than the smoky tem-
        ples,
Louder and harsher than the foamy sea.

Waiting among the rifled branches for the sun, our
        hero,
Sing, wind, too tuneless in the slender trees!

FOR MY BROTHER:
REPORTED MISSING IN ACTION, 1943

Sweet brother, if I do not sleep
My eyes are flowers for your tomb;
And if I cannot eat my bread,
My fasts shall live like willows where you died.
If in the heat I find no water for my thirst,
My thirst shall turn to springs for you, poor traveller.

Where, in what desolate and smokey country,
Lies your poor body, lost and dead?
And in what landscape of disaster
Has your unhappy spirit lost its road?

Come, in my labor find a resting place
And in my sorrows lay your head,
Or rather take my life and blood
And buy yourself a better bed—
Or take my breath and take my death
And buy yourself a better rest.

When all the men of war are shot
And flags have fallen into dust,
Your cross and mine shall tell men still
Christ died on each, for both of us.

12

For in the wreckage of your April Christ lies slain,
And Christ weeps in the ruins of my spring:
The money of Whose tears shall fall
Into your weak and friendless hand,
And buy you back to your own land:

The silence of Whose tears shall fall
Like bells upon your alien tomb.
Hear them and come: they call you home.

THE WINTER'S NIGHT

When, in the dark, the frost cracks on the window
The children awaken, and whisper.
One says the moonlight grated like a skate
Across the freezing river.
Another hears the starlight breaking like a knifeblade
Upon the silent, steelbright pond.
They say the trees are stiller than the frozen water
From waiting for a shouting light, a heavenly mes-
    sage.

Yet it is far from Christmas, when a star
Sang in the pane, as brittle as their innocen el!
For now the light of early Lent
Glitters upon the icy step—
"We have wept letters to our patron saints,
(The children say) yet slept before they ended."

Oh, is there in this night no sound of strings, of
    singers?
None coming from the wedding, no, nor Bride-
    groom's messenger?
(The sleepy virgins stir, and trim their lamps.)

The moonlight rings upon the ice as sudden as a
    footstep;
Starlight clinks upon the dooryard stone, too like a
    latch,
And the children are, again, awake,
And all call out in whispers to their guardian angels.

IN MEMORY OF THE SPANISH POET
FEDERICO GARCIA LORCA

Where the white bridge rears up its stamping arches
Proud as a colt across the clatter of the shallow river,
The sharp guitars
Have never forgotten your name.

Only the swordspeech of the cruel strings
Can pierce the minds of those who remain,
Sitting in the eyeless ruins of the houses,
The shelter of the broken wall.

A woman has begun to sing:
O music the color of olives!

Her eyes are darker than the deep cathedrals;
Her words come dressed as mourners,
In the gate of her shadowy voice,
Each with a meaning like a sheaf of seven blades!

The spires and high Giraldas, still as nails
Nailed in the four cross roads,
Watch where the song becomes the color of carna-
tions,
And flowers like wounds in the white dust of Spain.

(Under what crossless Calvary lie your lost bones,
Garcia Lorca?
What white Sierra hid your murder in a rocky val-
ley?)

In the four quarters of the world, the wind is still,
And wonders at the swordplay of the fierce guitar;
The voice has turned to iron in the naked air,
More loud and more despairing than a ruined tower.

(Under what crossless Calvary lie your lost bones,
Garcia Lorca?
What white Sierra hid your murder in a rocky val-
ley?)

THE TRAPPIST ABBEY: MATINS

(Our Lady of Gethsemani, Kentucky)

When the full fields begin to smell of sunrise
And the valleys sing in their sleep,
The pilgrim moon pours over the solemn darkness
Her waterfalls of silence,
And then departs, up the long avenue of trees.

The stars hide, in the glade, their light, like tears,
And tremble where some train runs, lost,
Baying in eastward mysteries of distance,
Where fire flares, somewhere, over a sink of cities.

Now kindle in the windows of this ladyhouse, my
        soul,
Your childish, clear awakeness:
Burn in the country night
Your wise and sleepless lamp.
For, from the frowning tower, the windy belfry,
Sudden the bells come, bridegrooms,
And fill the echoing dark with love and fear.

Wake in the windows of Gethsemani, my soul, my
        sister,
For the past years, with smokey torches, come,
Bringing betrayal from the burning world
And bloodying the glade with pitch flame.

Wake in the cloisters of the lonely night, my soul, my
    sister,
Where the apostles gather, who were, one time, scat-
    tered,
And mourn God's blood in the place of His betrayal,
And weep with Peter at the triple cock-crow.

EVENING

Now, in the middle of the limpid evening,
The moon speaks clearly to the hill.
The wheatfields make their simple music,
Praise the quiet sky.

And down the road, the way the stars come home,
The cries of children
Play on the empty air, a mile or more,
And fall on our deserted hearing,
Clear as water.

They say the sky is made of glass,
They say the smiling moon's a bride.
They say they love the orchards and apple trees,
The trees, their innocent sisters, dressed in blossoms,
Still wearing, in the blurring dusk,
White dresses from that morning's first communion.

And, where blue heaven's fading fire last shines
They name the new come planets
With words that flower
On little voices, light as stems of lilies.

And where blue heaven's fading fire last shines,
Reflected in the poplar's ripple,
One little, wakeful bird
Sings like a shower.

ARIADNE AT THE LABYRINTH

Patient, in the fire of noon,
Hands, that hold the thread, crossed,
Ariadne's a Barbadian flower,
And grows by the Labyrinth door.

Under the blue, airy-waters of evening,
Hands folded like white petals,
Watching for the bold adventurer,
Ariadne waits as calm as coral,
Silent as some plant of undersea.

Drums ring at the city's edge:
The speechless hills put on crowns of dark flame;
Dancing citizens fly like little flags
Amid the glad volcano of their congas.
But Ariadne's eyes are lakes
Beside the maze's starwhite wall:

For in the Carribbean midnight
Of her wild and gentle wisdom, she foreknows
And solves the maze's cruel algebra.

But when white morning
Runs with a shout along the jagged mountains
Strength of a cotton thread draws out to Ariadne
The Bravest Soldier, the Wisest Judge,
The Mightiest King!

ST. AGNES: A RESPONSORY

Cujus pulchritudinem
Sol et luna mirantur . . .
    Hear with what joy this child of God
    Plays in the perfect garden of her martyrdom,
Ipsi soli servo fidem.

    Spending the silver of her little life
    To bring her Bridegroom these bright flowers
    Of which her arms are full.

Cujus pulchritudinem . . .
    With what white smiles
    She buys the Popes their palliums,
    And lavishes upon our souls the lambs of her con-
        fession!
Sol et luna mirantur,
Ipsi soli servo fidem.

Her virtues, with their simple strings,
Play to the Lover hidden in the universe,
Cujus pulchritudinem . . .
Who smiles into the sun His looking-glass,
And fills it with His glorious face:
Who utters the round moon's recurring O
And drowns our dusks in peace.
Ipsi soli servo fidem!

The Roman captain's work is done:
Now he may tear his temples down—
Her charity has flown to four horizons, like the
swiftest doves,

Where all towns sing like springtime, with their new-
born bells
Pouring her golden name out of their crucibles.

SONG

from Crossportion's Pastoral

The bottom of the sea has come
And builded in my noiseless room
The fishes' and the mermaids' home,

Whose it is most, most hell to be
Out of the heavy-hanging sea
And in the thin, thin changeable air

Or unroom sleep some other where;
But play their coral violins
Where waters most look music in:

The bottom of my room, the sea.
Full of voiceless curtaindeep
There mermaid somnambules come sleep
Where fluted half-lights show the way,

And there, there lost orchestras play
And down the many quarterlights come
To the dim mirth of my aquadrome:
The bottom of my sea, the room.

THE MAN IN THE WIND

Here is the man who fancies Arab ponies,
Captain April, walking like the wind,
Breeding the happy swordlight of the sun.

Secret, in his looks and manner,
He's not as inattentive to the music as he seems,
That jangles in the empty doorways.

But his well-tempered spirit,
Rapt in the middle of a harmony,
Flies to a breathless wedding with the Palisades.

Then his five senses, separate as their numbers,
Scatter, like birds, from in front of his steps,
And instantly return, like water,
To the common Bermuda of the flashing river.

The mathematics of the air describes a perfect silence,
And Captain April's mind, leaning out of its own
    amazing windows,
Dies in a swirl of doves.

ARIADNE

All through the blazing afternoon
The hand drums talk together like locusts;
The flute pours out its endless, thin stream,
Threading it in and out the clatter of sticks upon
    wood-blocks.
Drums and bells exchange handfuls of bright coins,
Drums and bells scatter their music, like pennies, all
    over the air,
And see, the lutanist's thin hand
Rapidly picks the spangling notes off from his wires
And throws them about like drops of water.

Behind the bamboo blinds,
Behind the palms,
In the green, sundappled apartments of her palace
Redslippered Ariadne, with a tiny yawn,
Tosses a ball upon her roulette wheel.

Suddenly, dead north,
A Greek ship leaps over the horizon, skips like a colt,
    paws the foam.
The ship courses through the pasture of bright ame-
    thysts
And whinnies at the jetty.
The whole city runs to see:
Quick as closing your hand
The racing sail's down.
Then the drums are stunned, and the crowd, exalted,
    cries:
O Theseus! O Grecian hero!

Like a thought through the mind
Ariadne moves to the window.
Arrows of light, in every direction,
Leap from the armor of the black-eyed captain.
Arrows of light
Resound within her like the strings of a guitar.

TROPICS

At noon the sky goes off like a gun.

Guards, on the Penal Island,
Converging, mad as murder, in the swearing cane,
Arrest the four-footed wind.

But the chained and numbered men
Do not cease their labor:
Building a cage for the devouring sun.

At six o'clock exactly,
The day explodes like a bomb,
And it is night.

Instantly, the guards
Hide in the jungle, build a boat
And escape.

But the prisoners of the state
Do not cease their labor:
Collecting the asphalt fragments of the night.

ASH WEDNESDAY

The naked traveller,
Stretching, against the iron dawn, the bowstrings of
    his eyes,
Starves on the mad sierra.

But the sleepers,
Prisoners in a lovely world of weeds,
Make a small, red cry,
And change their dreams.

Proud as the mane of the whinnying air,
Yet humble as the flakes of water
Or the chips of the stone sun, the traveller
Is nailed to the hill by the light of March's razor;

And when the desert barks, in a rage of love
For the noon of the eclipse,
He lies with his throat cut, in a frozen crater.

Then the sleepers,
Prisoners of a moonward power of tides,
Slain by the stillness of their own reflections,
Sit up, in their graves, with a white cry,
And die of terror at the traveller's murder.

CRUSOE

Sometimes the sun beats up the rocks of capes
And robs the green world with a clangor of banks.

Then the citizens
Come out to stone the sky; and with their guns
Mean to shoot the highpowered spheres to pieces:
At dawn, the laws, in the yards of all the prisons,
Propose to hang the robber, the breeder of life.

What if no more men will learn to turn again
And run to the rainy world's boundaries?
What if no more men will learn to atone

By hard, horseplay of shipwreck in the drench of Ma-
    gellan,
And still steer by the stars' unending Lent?

What if the last man
Will no more learn, and run
The stern, foundering ocean, north of the line,
Where crew and cargo drown in the thrash of the
    wreck,
The day he's driven to his Penal Island,
His own rich acre of island, like the wiseguy Crusoe!

APRIL

April, like a leopard in the windy woods,
Sports with the javelins of the weather;

And the hunters,
Eye-level with the world's clean brim,
Sight their strings, in masking rocks not moving,
And shower with arrows
The innocent, immortal season.

Hear how like lights these following releases
Of sharpened shaft-flights sing across the air,
And play right through, unwounding, clearest wind-
    works—

To disappear, unpublished, in the reeds.

But where their words are quenched, the world is
    quickened:
The lean air suddenly flowers,
The little voices of the rivers change;

So that the hunters put away their silver quivers,
Die to the level of river and rockbrim,
And are translated, homeward,
To the other, solemn, world.

THE GREEK WOMEN

The ladies in red capes and golden bracelets
Walk like reeds and talk like rivers,
And sigh, like Vichy water, in the doorways;

And looks run down the land like colts,
Race with the wind, (the mares, their mothers', lover)
Down to the empty harbor.

All spine and sandal stand the willow women;
They shake their silver bangles
In the olive-light of clouds and windows,
Talking, among themselves, like violins;

And, opening their eyes wide as horizons,
Seem to await the navy home from Troy.

No longer stand together, widow women!
Give your gold ornaments to the poor,
Make run the waterspeech of beads between **your**
    fingers:
For Troy is burned, and Greece is cursed,
The plague comes like a cloud.
All your men are sleeping in the alien earth,

But one.
And Clytemnestra, walking like a willow, stares.
Beads and bracelets gently knifeclash all about her,
Because the conqueror, the homecome hero,
The soldier, Agamemnon,
Bleeds in her conscience, twisting like a root.

CALYPSO'S ISLAND

See with how little motion, now, the noon wind
Fills the woods' eyes with flirting oleanders,
While perpendicular sun lets fall
Nickels and dimes on the deep harbor.

Fair cries of divers fly in the air
Amid the rigging of the newcome schooner,
And the white ship
Rides like a petal on the purple water
And flings her clangorous anchor in the quiet deeps,
And wrecks the waving waterlights.

Then Queen Calypso
Wakes from a dreaming lifetime in her house of
    wicker,
Sees all at once the shadows on the matting
Coming and going like a leopard;
Hears for the first time the flame-feathered birds
Shout their litany in the savage tree;

And slowly tastes the red red wound
Of the sweet pomegranate,

And lifts her eyelids like the lids of treasures.

THE OHIO RIVER—LOUISVILLE

No one can hear the loud voice of the city
Because of the tremendous silence
Of this slow-moving river, quiet as space.

Not the towering bridge, the crawling train,
Not the knives of pylons
Clashing in the sun,
And not the sky-swung cables;
Not the outboard boat
Swearing in the fiery distance like a locust,
Not the iron cries of men:
Nothing is heard,
Only the immense and silent movement of the river.

The trains go through the summer quiet as paper,
And, in the powerhouse, the singing dynamos
Make no more noise than cotton.
All life is quieter than the weeds
On which lies lightly sprawling,
Like white birds shot to death,
The bathers' clothing.

But only where the swimmers float like alligators,
And with their eyes as dark as creosote
Scrutinize the murderous heat,
Only there is anything heard:
The thin, salt voice of violence,
That whines, like a mosquito, in their simmering
    blood.

THE HOUSE OF CAIPHAS

Somewhere, inside the wintry colonnade,
Stands, like a churchdoor statue, God's Apostle,
Good St. Peter, by the brazier,
With his back turned to the trial.

As scared and violent as flocks of birds of prey,
The testimonies of the holy beggars
Fly from the stones, and scatter in the windy shadows.

The accusations of the holy judge
Rise, in succession, dignified as rockets,

Soar out of silence to their towering explosions
And, with their meteors, raid the earth.

And the gates of night fall shut with the clangor of
arms.

The crafty eyes of witnesses, set free to riot,
Now shine as sharp as needles at the carved Apostle's
mantle.
Voices begin to rise, like water, in the colonnade;
Fingers accuse him like a herd of cattle.

Then the Apostle, white as marble, weak as tin
Cries out upon the crowd:
And, no less artificial than the radios of his voice,
He flees into the freezing night.

And all the constellations vanish out of heaven
With a glassy cry;
Cocks crow as sharp as steel in the terrible, clear east,

And the gates of night fall shut with the thunder of
Massbells.

AUBADE—HARLEM

(For Baroness C. de Hueck)

Across the cages of the keyless aviaries,
The lines and wires, the gallows of the broken kites,
Crucify; against the fearful light,
The ragged dresses of the little children.
Soon, in the sterile jungles of the waterpipes and
    ladders,
The bleeding sun, a bird of prey, will terrify the poor,
Who will forget the unbelievable moon.

But in the cells and wards of whiter buildings,
Where the glass dawn is brighter than the knives of
    surgeons,
Paler than alcohol or ether,
Greyer than guns and shinier than money,
The white men's wives, like Pilate's,
Cry in the peril of their frozen dreams:

"Daylight has driven iron spikes,
Into the flesh of Jesus' hands and feet:
Four flowers of blood have nailed Him to the walls
    of Harlem."

Along the white walls of the clinics and the hospitals
Pilate vanishes with a cry:
They have cut down two hundred Judases,
Hanged by the neck in the opera houses and mu-
    seums.

Across the cages of the keyless aviaries,
The lines and wires, the gallows of the broken kites,
Crucify, against the fearful light,
The ragged dresses of the little children.

DIRGE FOR A TOWN IN FRANCE

Up among the stucco pears, the iron vines,
Mute as their watered roses, their mimosas,
The wives gaze down among the traceries
Of balconies: the one-time finery
Of iron, suburban balconies.

Down in the shadowy doors,
Men fold their arms,
And hearken after the departing day
That somewhere sings more softly
Than merry-go-rounds in distant fairs.

O, it is not those first, faint stars
Whose fair light, falling, whispers in the river;
And it is not the dusty wind,
Waving the waterskirts of the shy-talking fountain,

That wakes the wooden horses' orchestra,
The fifing goldfinch, and the phony flute,
And the steam robins and electric nightingales
That blurred the ding of cymbals,

That other time, when childhood turned and turned
As grave as sculpture in a zodiac.

And yet the mystery comes on
Spontaneous as the street-lights, in the plane trees:
The trees, whose paint falls off in flakes,
Elaborate as the arches
Of a deserted opera!

The roses and mimosas in the windows
Adore the night they breathe, not understanding;
The women dream of bread and chocolate
In their aquariums
Of traceries, and lace, and cherubim;

But the men die, down in the shadowy doors,
The way their thoughts die in their eyes,
To see those sad and funny children
Run down the colonnade of trees
Where the carnival doesn't exist:

Those children, who are lost too soon,
With fading laughter, on the road along the river:
Gone, like the slowing cavalcade, the homeward
    horses.

AUBADE—THE CITY

Now that the clouds have come like cattle
To the cold waters of the city's river,
All the windows turn their scandalized expression
Toward the tide's tin dazzle,

And question, with their weak-eyed stare,
The riotous sun.

From several places at a time
Cries of defiance,
As delicate as frost, as sharp as glass,
Rise from the porcelain buildings
And break in the blue sky.

Then, falling swiftly from the air,
The fragments of this fragile indignation
Ring on the echoing streets
No louder than a shower of pins.

But suddenly the bridges' choiring cables
Jangle gently in the wind
And play like quiet piano-strings.

All down the faces of the buildings
Windows begin to close
Like figures in a long division.

Those whose eyes all night have simulated sleep,
Suddenly stare, from where they lie, like wolves,
Tied in the tangle of the bedding,

And listen for the waking blood
To flood the apprehensive silence of their flesh.
They fear the heart that now lies quenched may
    quicken,
And start to romp against the rib,
Soft and insistent as a secret bell.

They also fear the light will grow
Into the windows of their hiding places, like a tree
Of tropical flowers
And put them, one by one, to flight.

Then life will have to begin.
Pieces of paper, lying in the streets,
Will start up, in the twisting wind,
And fly like idiot birds before the faces of the crowds.
And in the roaring buildings
Elevator doors will have begun
To clash like sabres.

THE PERIL

When anger comes to the coast of our desolate country
And the sky is the color of armor,
We listen, in the silence of the cliffs and bays as still as
    steel,
For the cry that terrifies the sentinel.
And if it sound, oh! suddener than Java dancers
Face us all the swords we fear.
Well, we have arms: we will put them to trial.

But even as we wait, in hiding, for the unknown sig-
    nal,
It is the Bridegroom comes like lightning where we
    never looked!
His eyes are angels, armed in smiles of fire.
His Word puts out the spark of every other sun
Faster than sunlight ever hid the cities
Of the fire-crowded universe!
How shall I stand such light, being dim as my fear?

Rob me, and make me poor enough to bear my price-
    less ransom;
Lock me and dower me in the gifts and jails of tribu-
    lation:
Stab me and save me with the five lights of Your
    Crucifixion!

And I'll become as strong as wax, as weak as dia-
    monds,
And read Your speeches deeper than the sea
And, like the sky, fair!

ADVENT

Charm with your stainlessness these winter nights,
Skies, and be perfect!
Fly vivider in the fiery dark, you quiet meteors,
And disappear.
You moon, be slow to go down,
This is your full!

The four white roads make off in silence
Towards the four parts of the starry universe.
Time falls like manna at the corners of the wintry
    earth.
We have become more humble than the rocks,
More wakeful than the patient hills.

Charm with your stainlessness these nights in Advent,
    holy spheres,
While minds, as meek as beasts,
Stay close at home in the sweet hay;
And intellects are quieter than the flocks that feed by
    starlight.

Oh pour your darkness and your brightness over all
    our solemn valleys,
You skies: and travel like the gentle Virgin,
Toward the planets' stately setting,

Oh white full moon as quiet as Bethlehem!

CAROL

Flocks feed by darkness with a noise of whispers,
In the dry grass of pastures,
And lull the solemn night with their weak bells.

The little towns upon the rocky hills
Look down as meek as children:
Because they have seen come this holy time.

God's glory, now, is kindled gentler than low candle-
    light
Under the rafters of a barn:
Eternal Peace is sleeping in the hay,
And Wisdom's born in secret in a straw-roofed stable.

And O! Make holy music in the stars, you happy an-
    gels.
You shepherds, gather on the hill.
Look up, you timid flocks, where the three kings
Are coming through the wintry trees;

While we unnumbered children of the wicked cen-
turies
Come after with our penances and prayers,
And lay them down in the sweet-smelling hay
Beside the wise men's golden jars.

THE CANDLEMAS PROCESSION

Lumen
Ad revelationem gentium.

Look kindly, Jesus, where we come,
New Simeons, to kindle,
Each at Your infant sacrifice his own life's candle.

And when Your flame turns into many tongues,
See how the One is multiplied, among us, hundreds!
And goes among the humble, and consoles our sinful
kindred.

It is for this we come,
And, kneeling, each receive one flame:
Ad revelationem gentium.

Our lives, like candles, spell this simple symbol:

Weep like our bodily life, sweet work of bees,
Sweeten the world, with your slow sacrifice.
And this shall be our praise:
That by our glad expense, our Father's will
Burned and consumed us for a parable.

Nor burn we now with brown and smoky flames, but
    bright
Until our sacrifice is done,
(By which not we, but You are known)
And then, returning to our Father, one by one,
Give back our lives like wise and waxen lights.

CANA

"This beginning of miracles did Jesus
  in Cana of Galilee."

Once when our eyes were clean as noon, our rooms
Filled with the joys of Cana's feast:
For Jesus came, and His disciples, and His Mother,
And after them the singers
And some men with violins.

Once when our minds were Galilees,
And clean as skies our faces,
Our simple rooms were charmed with sun.

Our thoughts went in and out in whiter coats than
    God's disciples',
In Cana's crowded rooms, at Cana's tables.

Nor did we seem to fear the wine would fail:
For ready, in a row, to fill with water and a miracle,
We saw our earthen vessels, waiting empty.
What wine those humble waterjars foretell!

Wine for the ones who, bended to the dirty earth,
Have feared, since lovely Eden, the sun's fire,
Yet hardly mumble, in their dusty mouths, one prayer.

Wine for old Adam, digging in the briars!

ST. PAUL

When I was Saul, and sat among the cloaks,
My eyes were stones, I saw no sight of heaven,
Open to take the spirit of the twisting Stephen.
When I was Saul, and sat among the rocks,
I locked my eyes, and made my brain my tomb,
Sealed with what boulders rolled across my reason!

When I was Saul and walked upon the blazing desert
My road was quiet as a trap.
I feared what word would split high noon with light
And lock my life, and try to drive me mad:
And thus I saw the Voice that struck me dead.

Tie up my breath, and wind me in white sheets of
    anguish,
And lay me in my three days' sepulchre
Until I find my Easter in a vision.

Oh Christ! Give back my life, go, cross Damascus,
Find out my Ananias in that other room:
Command him, as you do, in this my dream;
He knows my locks, and owns my ransom,
Waits for Your word to take his keys and come.

TRAPPISTS, WORKING

Now all our saws sing holy sonnets in this world of
    timber
Where oaks go off like guns, and fall like cataracts,
Pouring their roar into the wood's green well.

Walk to us, Jesus, through the wall of trees,
And find us still adorers in these airy churches,
Singing our other Office with our saws and axes.
Still teach Your children in the busy forest,
And let some little sunlight reach us, in our mental
    shades, and leafy studies.

When time has turned the country white with grain
And filled our regions with the thrashing sun,
Walk to us, Jesus, through the walls of wheat

When our two tractors come to cut them down:
Sow some light winds upon the acres of our spirit,
And cool the regions where our prayers are reapers,
And slake us, Heaven, with Your living rivers.

ST. ALBERIC

When your loud axe's echo on the ponds, at early
morning,
Scared the shy mallard from the shallows grey as tin,
The glades gave back your hammers' antiphons—
The din of nails that shamed the lazy spring.
Striving, like Adam, with the barren wildwood,
And with the desolation of the brake,
You builded, in a reedy place
A cloister and a Ladychurch.

But when the stones and clean-hewn beams
Heard no more sounds but of the bees, your thought-
ful eyes
Were always full of exile,
Though peaceful with the peace of pilgrims, and with
happiness
That shamed, in the deep wood, the sentimental doves.

When in the church your canticles were done,
Even your silences were better than the birds, whose
song

Still fell, like fountains, from the forest to your sunny
    cloister.
And when, in the high-noon of contemplation, reason
    died by blindness,
Your faith escaped, and found the flowering Cross—
Loving, in Christ, the agony of Adam:
Body and Spirit tilled and gardened with our penances
    and death.

And from the flowers of that frightful Paradise,
(The wounds that heal the loving mind)
Your diligence could draw such excellence
As shamed the bees at work in the wild rock.

Then did you fill the cloisters of your intellect,
The tabernacles in the secret churches of your will.
Slowly you built sweet counsel, like a honeycomb,
And fed your life with living Wisdom, Heaven's es-
    sence.

THE BIOGRAPHY

Oh read the verses of the loaded scourges,
And what is written in their terrible remarks:
"The Blood runs down the walls of Cambridge town,
As useless as the waters of the narrow river—
While pub and alley gamble for His vesture."

Although my life is written on Christ's Body like a
    map,
The nails have printed in those open hands
More than the abstract names of sins,
More than the countries and the towns,
The names of streets, the numbers of the houses,
The record of the days and nights,
When I have murdered Him in every square and
    street.

Lance and thorn, and scourge and nail
Have more than made His Flesh my chronicle.
My journeys more than bite His bleeding feet.

Christ, from my cradle, I had known You everywhere,
And even though I sinned, I walked in You, and knew
    You were my world:
You were my France and England,
My seas and my America:
You were my life and air, and yet I would not own
    You.

Oh, when I loved You, even while I hated You,
Loving and yet refusing You in all the glories of Your
    universe

It was Your living Flesh I tore and trampled, not the
    air and earth:
Not that You feel us, in created things,
But knowing You, in them, made every sin a sacrilege;

And every act of greed became a desecration,
Spoiled and dishonored You as in Your Eucharist.

And yet with every wound You robbed me of a crime,
And as each blow was paid with Blood,
You paid me also each great sin with greater graces.
For even as I killed You,
You made Yourself a greater thief than any in Your
    company,
Stealing my sins into Your dying life,
Robbing me even of my death.

Where, on what cross my agony will come
I do not ask You:
For it is written and accomplished here,
On every Crucifix, on every altar.
It is my narrative that drowns and is forgotten
In Your five open Jordans,
Your voice that cries my: *"Consummatum est."*

If on Your Cross Your life and death and mine are
    one,
Love teaches me to read, in You, the rest of a new
    history.
I trace my days back to another childhood,
Exchanging, as I go,
New York and Cuba for Your Galilee,
And Cambridge for Your Nazareth,
Until I come again to my beginning,
And find a manger, star and straw,

A pair of animals, some simple men,
And thus I learn that I was born,
Now not in France, but Bethlehem.

AFTER THE NIGHT OFFICE—
GETHSEMANI ABBEY

It is not yet the grey and frosty time
When barns ride out of the night like ships:
We do not see the Brothers, bearing lanterns,
Sink in the quiet mist,
As various as the spirits who, with lamps, are sent
To search our souls' Jerusalems
Until our houses are at rest
And minds enfold the Word, our Guest.

Praises and canticles anticipate
Each day the singing bells that wake the sun,
But now our psalmody is done.
Our hasting souls outstrip the day:
Now, before dawn, they have their noon.
The Truth that transsubstantiates the body's night
Has made our minds His temple-tent:
Open the secret eye of faith
And drink these deeps of invisible light.

The weak walls
Of the world fall
And heaven, in floods, comes pouring in:

Sink from your shallows, soul, into eternity,
And slake your wonder at that deep-lake spring.
We touch the rays we cannot see,
We feel the light that seems to sing.

Go back to bed, red sun, you are too late,
And hide behind Mount Olivet—
For like the flying moon, held prisoner,
Within the branches of a juniper,
So in the cages of our consciousness
The Dove of God is prisoner yet:
Unruly sun, go back to bed.

But now the lances of the morning
Fire all their gold against the steeple and the water-
    tower.
Returning to the windows of our deep abode of peace,
Emerging at our conscious doors
We find our souls all soaked in grace, like Gedeon's
    fleece.

THE TRAPPIST CEMETERY—
GETHSEMANI

Brothers, the curving grasses and their daughters
Will never print your praises:
The trees our sisters, in their summer dresses,

Guard your fame in these green cradles:
The simple crosses are content to hide your characters.

Oh do not fear
The birds that bicker in the lonely belfry
Will ever give away your legends.
Yet when the sun, exulting like a dying martyr,
Canonizes, with his splendid fire, the sombre hills,
Your graves all smile like little children,
And your wise crosses trust the mothering night
That folds them in the Sanctuary's wings.

You need not hear the momentary rumors of the road
Where cities pass and vanish in a single car
Filling the cut beside the mill
With roar and radio,
Hurling the air into the wayside branches
Leaving the leaves alive with panic.

See, the kind universe,
Wheeling in love about the abbey steeple,
Lights up your sleepy nursery with stars.

*　*　*

God, in your bodily life,
Untied the snares of anger and desire,
Hid your flesh from envy by these country altars,
Beneath these holy eaves where even sparrows have
      their houses.
But oh, how like the swallows and the chimney swifts
Do your free souls in glory play!
And with a cleaner flight,

Keener, more graceful circles,
Rarer and finer arcs
Than all these innocent attacks that skim our steeple!
How like these children of the summer evening
Do your rejoicing spirits
Deride the dry earth with their aviation!

But now the treble harps of night begin to play in the
     deep wood,
To praise your holy sleep,
And all the frogs along the creek
Chant in the moony waters to the Queen of Peace.
And we, the mariners, and travellers,
The wide-eyed immigrants,
Praying and sweating in our steerage cabins,
Lie still and count with love the measured bells
That tell the deep-sea leagues until your harbor.

Already on this working earth you knew what name-
     less love
Adorns the heart with peace by night,
Hearing, adoring all the dark arrivals of eternity.
Oh, here on earth you knew what secret thirst
Arming the mind with instinct,
Answers the challenges of God with garrisons
Of unified desire
And facing Him in His new wars
Is slain at last in an exchange of lives.

Teach us, Cistercian Fathers, how to wear
Silence, our humble armor.
Pray us a torrent of the seven spirits

That are our wine and stamina:
Because your work is not yet done.
But look: the valleys shine with promises,
And every burning morning is a prophecy of Christ
Coming to raise and vindicate
Even our sorry flesh.

Then will your graves, Gethsemani, give up their
    angels,
Return them to their souls to learn
The songs and attitudes of glory.
Then will creation rise again like gold
Clean, from the furnace of your litanies:
The beasts and trees shall share your resurrection,
And a new world be born from these green tombs.

LA SALETTE

It is a hundred years since your shy feet
Ventured to stand upon the pasture grass of the high
    Alps,
Coming no deeper in our smoky atmosphere
Than these blue skies, the mountain eyes
Of the two shepherd children, young as flowers,
Born to be dazzled by no mortal snow.

Lady, it is a hundred years
Since those fair, terrible tears
Reproved, with their amazing grief

All the proud candor of those altitudes:
Crowning the flowers at your feet
With diamonds, that seized upon, transfigured into
    nails of light
The rays of the mountain sun!—

And by their news,
(Which came with cowbells to the evening village
And to the world with church-bells
After not too many days,)
And by their news

We thought the walls of all hard hearts
Had broken down, and given in,
Poured out their dirty garrisons of sin,
And washed the streets with our own blood, if need
    be—
—Only to have them clean!

And though we did not understand
The weight and import of so great a sorrow,
We never thought so soon to have seen
The loss of its undying memory,
Passing from the black world without a word,
Without a funeral!
For while our teeth were battling in the meat of mir-
    acles and favors,
Your words, your prophecies, were all forgotten!

Now, one by one,
The things you said
Have come to be fulfilled.

John, in the might of his Apocalypse, could not fore-
    tell
Half of the story of our monstrous century,
In which the arm of your inexorable Son,
Bound, by His Truth, to disavow your intercession
For this wolf-world, this craven zoo,
Has bombed the doors of hell clean off their hinges,
And burst the cage of antichrist,
And roused, with His first two great thunderbolts,
The chariots of Armageddon.

LANDSCAPE, PROPHET AND WILD-DOG

The trees stand like figures in a theatre.
Then suddenly there comes a prophet, running for his
    life,
And the wild-dog behind him.
And now the wild-dog has him by the ankle
And the man goes down.

"Oh prophet, when it was afternoon you told us:
'Tonight is the millenium,
The withering-away of the state.
The skies, in smiles, shall fold upon the world,
Melting all injustice in the rigors of their breezy
    love.'
And all night long we waited at the desert's edge,
Hearing this wild-dog, only, on the far mountain,
Watching the white moon giggle in the stream!"

The two trees stand like Masters of Arts
And observe the wild-dog
Nailing his knives into the prophet's shoulder.

"Oh prophet, when it was night you came and
told us:
'Tomorrow is the mellenium,
The golden age!
The human race will wake up
And find dollars growing out of the palms of their
hands,
And the whole world will die of brotherly love
Because the factories jig like drums
And furnaces feed themselves,
And all men lie in idleness upon the quilted pas-
tures,
Tuning their friendly radios and dreaming in the
sun!"

"But when the grey day dawned
What flame flared in the jaws of the avenging
mills!
We heard the clash of hell within the gates of the
embattled Factory
And thousands died in the teeth of those sarcastic
fires!"

"And now the rivers are poisoned,
The skies rain blood
And all the springs are brackish with the taste
Of these your prophecies.

Oh prophet, tell us plainly, at last:
When is the day of our success?"

But there is no answer in the dead jaws.
And the air is full of wings.
The crows come down and sit like senators
On the arms of the two trees.

At the edge of the salt-lands
In the dry-blue clay
The wild-dog, with a red claw scuffs out a little hol-
    low,
Burying the prophet's meatless shin.

LANDSCAPE: BEAST

Yonder, by the eastward sea
Where smoke melts in a saucer of extinguished cities,
The last men stand, in delegations,
Waiting to see the seven-headed business
Promised us, from those unpublished deeps:
Waiting to see those horns and diadems
And hear the seven voices of the final blasphemy.

And westward, where the other waters are as slick as
    silk
And slide, in the grey evening, with uncertain lights,
(Screened by the smoke of the extinguished studios)

The last men wait to see the seven-headed thing.
They stand around the radios
Wearing their regalia on their thin excited breasts,
Waving the signals of their masonry.
What will happen, when they see those heads, those
    horns
Dishevel the flickering sea?

How will they bare their foreheads, and put forth
    their hands
And wince with the last indelible brand,
And wear the dolour of that animal's number,
And evermore be burned with her disgusting name?

Inland, in the lazy distance, where a dozen planes still
    play
As loud as horseflies, round the ruins of an average
    town,
A blue-green medium dragon, swimming in the river,
Emerges from the muddy waters, comes to romp
    awhile upon the land.
She rises on the pathless shore,
And goes to roll in the ashes of the ravaged country.
But no man turns to see and be surprised
Where those grey flanks flash palely in the sun.
Who shall gather to see an ordinary dragon, in this
    day of anger,
Or wonder at those scales as usual as sin?

Meanwhile, upon the broken mountains of the south
No one observes the angels passing to and fro:

And no one sees the fire that shoots beneath the hoofs
Of all the white, impatient horses.

And no one hears or fears the music of those blazing
    swords.

(Northward, northward, what lies there to see?
Who shall recount the terror of those ruined streets?

And who shall dare to look where all the birds with
    golden beaks
Stab at the blue eyes of the murdered saints?)

THE HEAVENLY CITY

City, when we see you coming down,
Coming down from God
To be the new world's crown:
How shall they sing, the fresh, unsalted seas
Hearing your harmonies!

For there is no more death,
No need to cure those waters, now, with any brine;
Their shores give them no dead,
Rivers no blood, no rot to stain them.

Because the cruel algebra of war
Is now no more.
And the steel circle of time, inexorable,

Bites like a padlock shut, forever,
In the smoke of the last bomb:
And in that trap the murderers and sorcerers and
crooked leaders
Go rolling home to hell.
And history is done.

Shine with your lamb-light, shine upon the world:
You are the new creation's sun.
And standing on their twelve foundations,
Lo, the twelve gates that are One Christ are wide as
canticles:
And Oh! Begin to hear the thunder of the songs
within the crystal Towers,
While all the saints rise from their earth with feet like
light
And fly to tread the quick-gold of those streets,

Oh, City, when we see you sailing down,
Sailing down from God,
Dressed in the glory of the Trinity, and angel-
crowned
In nine white diadems of liturgy.

THREE POSTCARDS FROM THE MONASTERY

I

The pilgrim passes swiftly.
All the strange towns,
Wrapped in their double cloaks
(Of rain and of non-entity)
Veil their elusive faces.

The pale world, white as plaster,
(Its doors are dumb, its windows far too blind for
    lamentation)
Dies like problematical news.

We have receded from the things
You printed on those unidentified facades.
We barely dream about the frontispiece
Of your collapsing palaces.
We can refuse your tin.

The smoky choirs
Of those far five-o'clock trombones
Have blown away. Our eyes
Are clean as the September night.
Our minds, (our silences) are light years deep.

Who shall amaze us with the noise of your discovery,
America?
Who shall make known to us your new, true name,
Instead of knocking at our gates,
Bidding us look again upon that blank and pictured
concentration?

Because the ticker-tapes are dead,
The radios are all shot:
But we have gone up to buy you Andromeda.

II

It is because the sun
Shines on the shallows like a cannonade
That we have come inland.

It is because the cloudy sea
Hailing the cliffs as loud as promises,
Saluting all the continent with foaming orchestras,

Raided the shore with tons of silver
That we have fled to the penniless hills,
Hidden in the poor, laborious fields.

We stood one moment by the bridgehead of those fatal
fortunes:
Days that offered to fill our hands with gold,
Surfs that crowded the grey rocks with ballyhoo.

Shall I speak plain against the sun?
Or sing together with the comic-operas of the sea?
We have refused the reward,
We have abandoned the man-hunt.
But when the contest is over
We shall inherit the world.

III

Once were begotten
In the wombs of the deep mountains:
Born over and over in the play of penitential tunnels.
Such was our birth and resurrection from the freezing
    east
The night we cleared you, Pittsburgh, in a maze of
    lights.

Our lives were suddenly weaned in strange Ohio,
(Whose towns made little love to us, in their green
    requiems)
Weaned from the land and atmosphere of men.

Have you ever heard this music
Sung over and over by night,
How we will live *in loco pascuae?*
Or the assuring voices of those inward violins
Play: "Going to Gethsemani?"

(We were begotten in the tunnels of December rain,
Born from the wombs of news and tribulation.
By night, by wakeful rosary:

Such was my birth, my resurrection from the freezing
    east,
The night we cleared you, Cincinnati, in a maze of
    lights.)

ON THE ANNIVERSARY OF MY BAPTISM

Certain waters are as blue as metal
Or as salt as sorrow.
Others wince like brass in the hammering sun,
Or stammer all over with tremors of shadow
That die as fast as the light winds
Whose flights surprise the promontories
And the marble bay.

Some are crowded everywhere, off-shore, with purple
    coral
Between the fleets of light that founder in the sand.
Others are full of yawls, or loud with launches,
Or sadder than the bitter smoke
Of tug and trawler, tramp and collier,

Or as grey as battle.

Oh! Since I was a baby in the Pyrenees,
When old St. Martin marked me for the cloister from
    high Canigou,

How many deeps, how many wicked seas
Went to befriend me with a flash of white-caps
Louder than laughter in the wind and sun,
Or sluggered all our brown bows gunwale-under
In their rowdy thunder—
Only to return me to the land.

Do you suppose that if the green Atlantic
Had ever cracked our brittle shell
And rifled all the cabins for their fruit of drunken
     passengers,
Do you suppose my sins,
Once we were sorted and disposed forever
Along the shelves of that profound, unvisited mu-
     seum,
Would there have been immune,
Or learned to keep their coats of unreality
From the deep sea's most patient candying?

The day You made the waters,
And dragged them down from the dividing islands
And made them spring with fish,
You planned to bless the brine out of the seas
That were to be my death.

And this is the ninth November since my world's end
     and my Genesis,
When, with the sting of salt in my dry mouth,
Cross-crowned with water by the priest,
Stunned at the execution of my old companion, death,

And with the murder of my savage history,
You drowned me in the shallow font.

My eyes, swimming in unexpected infancy,
Were far too frail for such a favor:
They still close-kept the stone shell of their empty
    sepulchre:
But, though they saw none, guessed the new-come
    Trinity
That charged my sinews with His secret life.

DUNS SCOTUS

Striking like lightning to the quick of the real world
Scotus has mined all ranges to their deepest veins:
But where, oh, on what blazing mountain of theology
And in what Sinai's furnace
Did God refine that gold?

Who ruled those arguments in their triumphant order
And armed them with their strict celestial light?
See the lance-lightning, blade-glitter, banner-progress
As love advances, company by company
In sunlit teams his clean embattled reasons,

Until the firmament, with high heavenly marvel
Views in our crystal souls her blue embodiment,
Unfurls a thousand flags above our heads—
It is the music of Our Lady's army!

For Scotus is her theologian,
Nor has there ever been a braver chivalry than his
    precision.
His thoughts are skies of cloudless peace
Bright as the vesture of her grand aurora
Filled with the rising Christ.

But we, a weak, suspicious generation,
Loving emotion, hating prayer,
We are not worthy of his wisdom.
Creeping like beasts between the mountain's feet
We look for laws in the Arabian dust.
We have no notion of his freedom

Whose acts despise the chains of choice and passion.
We have no love for his beatitude
Whose act renounces motion:
Whose love flies home forever
As silver as felicity,
Working and quiet in the dancelight of an everlasting
    arrow.

Lady, the image of whose heaven
Sings in the might of Scotus' reasoning:
There is no line of his that has not blazed your glory
    in the schools,
Though in dark words, without romance,
Calling us to swear you our liege.

Language was far too puny for his great theology:
But, oh! His thought strode through those words

Bright as the conquering Christ
Between the clouds His enemies:
And in the clearing storm and Sinai's dying thunder
Scotus comes out, and shakes his golden locks
And sings like the African sun.

EVENING: ZERO WEATHER

Now the lone world is streaky as a wall of marble
With veins of clear and frozen snow.
There is no bird-song there, no hare's track
No badger working in the russet grass:
All the bare fields are silent as eternity.

And the whole herd is home in the long barn.
The brothers come, with hoods about their faces,
Following their plumes of breath
Lugging the gleaming buckets one by one.

This was a day when shovels would have struck
Full flakes of fire out of the land like rock:
And ground cries out like iron beneath our boots

When all the monks come in with eyes as clean as the
    cold sky
And axes under their arms,
Still paying out *Ave Marias*
With rosaries between their bleeding fingers.

We shake the chips out of our robes outside the door
And go to hide in cowls as deep as clouds,
Bowing our shoulders in the church's shadow, lean
    and whipped,
To wait upon your Vespers, Mother of God!

And we have eyes no more for the dark pillars or the
    freezing windows,
Ears for the rumorous cloister or the chimes of time
    above our heads:
For we are sunken in the summer of our adoration,
And plunge, down, down into the fathoms of our
    secret joy
That swims with indefinable fire.

And we will never see the copper sunset
Linger a moment, like an echo, on the frozen hill
Then suddenly die an hour before the Angelus.

For we have found our Christ, our August
Here in the zero days before Lent—
We are already binding up our sheaves of harvest
Beating the lazy liturgy, going up with exultation
Even on the eve of our Ash Wednesday,
And entering our blazing heaven by the doors of the
    Assumption!

FREEDOM AS EXPERIENCE

When, as the captive of Your own invincible consent,
You love the image of Your endless Love,
Three-Personed God, what intellect
Shall take the measure of that liberty?

Compared with Love, Your Triune Law,
All the inexorable stars are anarchists:
Yet they are bound by Love and Love is infinitely free.

Minds cannot understand, nor systems imitate
The scope of such simplicity.
All the desires and hungers that defy Your Law
Wither to fears, and perish in imprisonment:
And all the hopes that seem to founder in the shadows
    of a cross
Wake from a momentary sepulchre, and they are
    blinded by their freedom!

Because our natures poise and point towards You
Our loves revolve about You as the planets swing
    upon the sun
And all suns sing together in their gravitational
    worlds.

And so, some days in prayer Your Love,
Prisoning us in darkness from the values of Your
    universe,

Delivers us from measure and from time,
Melts all the barriers that stop our passage to eternity
And solves the hours our chains.

And then, as fires like jewels germinate
Deep in the stone heart of a Kaffir mountain,
So now our gravity, our new-created deep desire
Burns in our life's mine like an undiscovered diamond.

Locked in that strength we stay and stay
And cannot go away
For You have given us our liberty.

Imprisoned in the fortunes of Your adamant
We can no longer move, for we are free.

THE SOWING OF MEANINGS

See the high birds! Is their's the song
That flies among the wood-light
Wounding the listener with such bright arrows?
Or do they play in wheeling silences
Defining in the perfect sky
The bounds of (here below) our solitude,

Where spring has generated lights of green
To glow in clouds upon the sombre branches?

Ponds full of sky and stillnesses
What heavy summer songs still sleep
Under the tawny rushes at your brim?

More than a season will be born here, nature,
In your world of gravid mirrors!
The quiet air awaits one note,
One light, one ray and it will be the angels' spring:
One flash, one glance upon the shiny pond, and then
Asperges me! sweet wilderness, and lo! we are re-
deemed!

For, like a grain of fire
Smouldering in the heart of every living essence
God plants His undivided power——
Buries His thought too vast for worlds
In seed and root and blade and flower,

Until, in the amazing light of April,
Surcharging the religious silence of the spring,
Creation finds the pressure of His everlasting secret
Too terrible to bear.

Then every way we look, lo! rocks and trees
Pastures and hills and streams and birds and firma-
ment
And our own souls within us flash, and shower us
with light,
While the wild countryside, unknown, unvisited of
men,
Bears sheaves of clean, transforming fire.

And then, oh then the written image, schooled in
    sacrifice,
The deep united threeness printed in our being,
Shot by the brilliant syllable of such an intuition,
    turns within,
And plants that light far down into the heart of dark-
    ness and oblivion,
Dives after, and discovers flame.

THE LANDFALL

We are beyond the ways of the far ships
Here in this coral port,
Farther than the ways of fliers,
Because our destinies have suddenly transported us
Beyond the brim of the enamel world.

O Mariner, what is the name of this uncharted Land?
On these clean shores shall stand what sinless voyager,
What angel breathe the music of this atmosphere?

Look where the thin flamingoes
Burning upon the purple shallows with their rare,
    pale flames,
Stand silent as our thought, although the birds in the
    high rock
Rinse our new senses with no mortal note,
What are these wings whose silks amaze the traveller?

The flowering palms charm all the strand
With their supernal scent.
The oleander and the wild hibiscus paint
The land with blood, and unknown blooms
Open to us the Gospel of their five wild wounds.

And the deep ferns sing this epithalame:
"Go up, go up! this desert is the door of heaven!
And it shall prove your frail soul's miracle!
Climb the safe mountain,

Disarm your labored flesh, and taste the treasure of
    these silences
In the high coral hermitage,
While the clean winds bemuse you in the clefted rock;
Or find you there some leafy Crusoe-castle: dwell in
    trees!

Take down the flagons of the blue and crimson fruits
And reap the everlasting wheat that no man's hand
    has sown,
And strike the rock that runs with waters strong as
    wine
To fill you with their fortitude:
Because this island is your Christ, your might, your
    fort, your paradise.

And lo! dumb time's grey, smoky argosies
Will never anchor in this emerald harbor
Or find this world of amber,
Spoil the fair music of the silver sea

Or foul these chiming amethysts:
Nor comes there any serpent near this isle trenched
    in deep ocean
And walled with innocent, flowering vines.

But from beyond the cotton clouds,
Between those lovely, white cathedrals full of sun,
The angels study beauty with their steps
And tread like notes of music down the beamy air
To gain this new world's virgin shore:
While from the ocean's jeweled floor
The long-lost divers, rising one by one,
Smile and throw down their dripping fortunes on the
    sand,

And sing us the strange tale
Of the drowned king (our nature), his return!

THE READER

Lord, when the clock strikes
Telling the time with cold tin
And I sit hooded in this lectern

Waiting for the monks to come,
I see the red cheeses, and bowls
All smile with milk in ranks upon their tables.

74

Light fills my proper globe
(I have won light to read by
With a little, tinkling chain)

And the monks come down the cloister
With robes as voluble as water.
I do not see them but I hear their waves.

It is winter, and my hands prepare
To turn the pages of the saints:
And to the trees Thy moon has frozen on the win-
    dows
My tongue shall sing Thy Scripture.

Then the monks pause upon the step
(With me here in this lectern
And Thee there on Thy crucifix)
And gather little pearls of water on their fingers' ends
Smaller than this my psalm.

ST. MALACHY

In November, in the days to remember the dead
When air smells cold as earth,
St. Malachy, who is very old, gets up,
Parts the thin curtains of trees and dawns upon our
    land.

His coat is filled with drops of rain, and he is bearded
With all the seas of Poseidon.

(Is it a crozier, or a trident in his hand?)
He weeps against the gothic window, and the empty
    cloister
Mourns like an ocean shell.

Two bells in the steeple
Talk faintly to the old stranger
And the tower considers his waters.
"I have been sent to see my festival," (his cavern
    speaks!)
"For I am the saint of the day.
Shall I shake the drops from my locks and stand in
    your transept,
Or, leaving you, rest in the silence of my history?"

So the bells rang and we opened the antiphoners
And the wrens and larks flew up out of the pages.
Our thoughts became lambs. Our hearts swam like
    seas.
One monk believed that we should sing to him
Some stone-age hymn
Or something in the giant language.
So we played to him in the plainsong of the giant
    Gregory:
Oceans of Scripture sang upon bony Eire.

Then the last salvage of flowers
(Fostered under glass after the gardens foundered)
Held up their little lamps on Malachy's altar
To peer into his wooden eyes before the Mass began.

Rain sighed down the sides of the stone church.
Storms sailed by all day in battle fleets.

At five o'clock, when we tried to see the sun, the
     speechless visitor
Sighed and arose and shook the humus from his feet
And with his trident stirred our trees
And left down-wood, shaking some drops upon the
     ground.

Thus copper flames fall, tongues of fire fall
The leaves in hundreds fall upon his passing
While night sends down her dreadnought darkness
Upon this spurious Pentecost.

And the Melchisedec of our year's end
Who came without a parent, leaves without a trace,
And rain comes rattling down upon our forest
Like the doors of a country jail.

THE CAPTIVES—A PSALM

*Quomodo cantabimus canticum Domini in terra
aliena?*

Somewhere a king walks in his gallery
Owning the gorges of a fiery city.
Brass traffic shakes the walls. The windows shiver
     with business.
It is the bulls' day. The citizens
Build themselves each hour another god
And fry a fatter idol out of mud.

They cut themselves a crooked idiom
To the winged animals, upon their houses.
Prayers are made of money, songs of numbers,
Hymns of the blood of the killed.

Old ladies are treasured in sugar.
Young ones rot in wine.
The flesh of the fat organizers smiles with oil.

Blessed is the army that will one day crush you, city,
Like a golden spider.
Blest are they that hate you. Blest are they
That dash your brats against the stones.

The children of God have died, O Babylon,
Of thy wild algebra.

Days, days are the journey
From wall to wall. And miles
Miles of houses shelter terror.
And we lie chained to their dry roots, O Israel!

Our bodies are greyer than mud.
There, butterflies are born to be dancers
And fly in black and blue along the drunken river
Where, in the willow trees, Assyria lynched our song!

May my bones burn and ravens eat my flesh
If I forget thee, contemplation!
May language perish from my tongue
If I do not remember thee, O Sion, city of vision,

Whose heights have windows finer than the firma-
    ment
When night pours down her canticles
And peace sings on thy watchtowers like the stars of
    Job.

IN THE RAIN AND THE SUN

Watch out for this peeled doorlight!
Here, without rain, without shame
My noonday dusk made spots upon the walk:
Tall drops pelted the concrete with their jewelry
Belonging to the old world's bones.

Owning this view, in the air of a hermit's weather,
I count the fragmentary rain
In drops as blue as coal
Until I plumb the shadows full of thunder.
My prayers supervise the atmosphere
Till storms call all hounds home.

Out of the towers of water
Four or five mountains come walking
To see the little monks' graves.
Flying the neutral stones I dwell between cedars
And see the countries sleeping in their beds:
Lands of the watermen, where poplars bend.

Wild seas amuse the world with water:
No end to all the surfs that charm our shores
Fattening the sands with their old foam and their old
    roar.

Thus in the boom of waves' advantage
Dogs and lions come to my tame home
Won by the bells of my Cistercian jungle.
O love the livid fringes
In which their robes are drenched!

Songs of the lions and whales!
With my pen between my fingers
Making the waterworld sing!
Sweet Christ, discover diamonds
And sapphires in my verse
While I burn the sap of my pine house
For praise of the ocean sun.

I have walked upon the whole days' surf
Rinsing Thy bays with hymns.
My eyes have swept horizons clean
Of ships and rain.
Upon the lacquered swells my feet no longer run.
Sliding all over the sea I come
To the hap of a slippery harbor.

Dogs have gone back to their ghosts
And the many lions, home.

But words fling wide the windows of their houses—
Adam and Eve walk down my coast
Praising the tears of the treasurer sun:

I hang Thy rubies on these autumn trees,
On the bones of the homegoing thunder.

DRY PLACES

No cars go by
Where dogs are barking at the desert.
Yet it is not twenty years since many lamps
Shed their juices in this one time town
And stores grew big lights, like oranges and pears.

Now not one lame miner
Sits on the rotten verandah,
Works in the irons where
Judas' shadow dwells.
Yet I could hew a city
From the side of their hill.

O deep stone covert where the dusk
Is full of lighted beasts
And the mad stars preach wars without end:
Whose bushes and grasses live without water,

There the skinny father of hate rolls in his dust
And if the wind should shift one leaf
The dead jump up and bark for their ghosts:
Their dry bones want our penniless souls.

Bones, go back to your baskets.
Get your fingers out of my clean skin.
Rest in your rainless death until your own souls
Come back in the appointed way and sort you out
        from your remains.

We who are still alive will wring a few green blades
From the floor of this valley
Though ploughs abhor your metal and your clay.
Rather than starve with you in rocks without oasis,

We will get up and work your loam
Until some prayer or some lean sentence
Bleeds like the quickest root they ever cut.

For we cannot forget the legend of the world's child-
        hood
Or the track to the dogwood valley
And Adam our Father's old grass farm
Wherein they gave the animals names
And knew Christ was promised first without scars
When all God's larks called out to Him
In their wild orchard.

A RESPONSORY, 1948

Suppose the dead could crown their wit
With some intemperate exercise,
Spring wine from their ivory
Or roses from their eyes?

Or if the wise could understand
And the world without heart
That the dead are not yet dead
And that the living live apart

And the wounded are healing,
Though in a place of flame.
The sick in a great ship
Are riding. They are riding home.

Suppose the dead could crown their wit
With some intemperate exercise,
Spring wine from their ivory
Or roses from their eyes?

Two cities sailed together
For many thousand years.
And now they drift asunder.
The tides of new wars

Sweep the sad heavens,
Divide the massed stars,
The black and white universe
The blooming spheres.

Down, down, down
The white armies fall
Moving their ordered snows
Toward the jaws of hell.

Suppose the dead could crown their wit
With some intemperate exercise,
Spring wine from their ivory
Or roses from their eyes?

A PSALM

When psalms surprise me with their music
And antiphons turn to rum
The Spirit sings: the bottom drops out of my soul

And from the center of my cellar, Love, louder than
    thunder
Opens a heaven of naked air.

New eyes awaken.
I send Love's name into the world with wings
And songs grow up around me like a jungle.
Choirs of all creatures sing the tunes
Your Spirit played in Eden.
Zebras and antelopes and birds of paradise
Shine on the face of the abyss
And I am drunk with the great wilderness
Of the sixth day in Genesis.

But sound is never half so fair
As when that music turns to air
And the universe dies of excellence.

Sun, moon and stars
Fall from their heavenly towers.
Joys walk no longer down the blue world's shore.

Though fires loiter, lights still fly on the air of the
    gulf,
All fear another wind, another thunder:
Then one more voice
Snuffs all their flares in one gust.

And I go forth with no more wine and no more stars
And no more buds and no more Eden
And no more animals and no more sea:

While God sings by himself in acres of night
And walls fall down, that guarded Paradise.

SENESCENTE MUNDO

Senescente mundo, when the hot globe
Shrivels and cracks
And uninhibited atoms resolve
Earth and water, fruit and flower, body and animal
    soul,
All the blue stars come tumbling down.

Beauty and ugliness and love and hate
Wisdom and politics are all alike undone.

Toward that fiery day we run like crabs
With our bad-tempered armor on.
"With blood and carpets, oranges and ashes,
Rubber and limes and bones,"
(So sing the children on the Avenue)
"With cardboard and dirty water and a few flames for
    the Peacelover's ghost,
We know where the dead bodies are
Studying the ceiling from the floors of their homes,
With smoke and roses, slate and wire
And crushed fruit and much fire."

Yet in the middle of this murderous season
Great Christ, my fingers touch Thy wheat
And hold Thee hidden in the compass of Thy paper
    sun.
There is no war will not obey this cup of Blood,
This wine in which I sink Thy words, in the anony-
    mous dawn!
I hear a Sovereign talking in my arteries
Reversing, with His Promises, all things
That now go on with fire and thunder.
His Truth is greater than disaster.
His Peace imposes silence on the evidence against us.

And though the world, at last, has swallowed her own
    solemn laughter
And has condemned herself to hell:

Suppose a whole new universe, a great clean Kingdom
Were to rise up like an Atlantis in the East,
Surprise this earth, this cinder, with new holiness!

Here in my hands I hold that secret Easter.
Tomorrow, this will be my Mass's answer,
Because of my companions whom the wilderness has
    eaten,
Crying like Jonas in the belly of our whale.

ELEGY FOR THE MONASTERY BARN

As though an aged person were to wear
Too gay a dress
And walk about the neighborhood
Announcing the hour of her death,

So now, one summer day's end,
At suppertime, when wheels are still,
The long barn suddenly puts on the traitor, beauty,
And hails us with a dangerous cry,
For: "Look!" she calls to the country,
"Look how fast I dress myself in fire!"

Had we half guessed how long her spacious shadows
Harbored a woman's vanity
We would be less surprised to see her now
So loved, and so attended, and so feared.

She, in whose airless heart
We burst our veins to fill her full of hay,
Now stands apart.
She will not have us near her. Terribly,
Sweet Christ, how terribly her beauty burns us now!

And yet she has another legacy,
More delicate, to leave us, and more rare.

Who knew her solitude?
Who heard the peace downstairs
While flames ran whispering among the rafters?
Who felt the silence, there,
The long, hushed gallery
Clean and resigned and waiting for the fire?

Look! They have all come back to speak their sum-
    mary:
Fifty invisible cattle, the past years
Assume their solemn places one by one.
This is the little minute of their destiny.
Here is their meaning found. Here is their end.

Laved in the flame as in a Sacrament
The brilliant walls are holy
In their first-last hour of joy.

Fly from within the barn! Fly from the silence
Of this creature sanctified by fire!
Let no man stay inside to look upon the Lord!
Let no man wait within and see the Holy
One sitting in the presence of disaster
Thinking upon this barn His gentle doom!

THE GUNS OF FORT KNOX

Guns at the camp (I hear them suddenly)
Guns make the little houses jump. I feel
Explosions in my feet, through boards.
Wars work under the floor. Wars
Dance in the foundations. Trees
Must also feel the guns they do not want
Even in their core.
As each charge bumps the shocked earth
They shudder from the root.

Shock the hills, you guns! They are
Not too firm even without dynamite.
These Chinese clayfoot hills
Founded in their own shale
Shift their feet in friable stone.

            Such ruins cannot
Keep the armies of the dead
From starting up again.
They'll hear these guns tonight
Tomorrow or some other time.
They'll wake. They'll rise
Through the stunned rocks, form
Regiments and do death's work once more.

Guns, I say, this is not
The right resurrection. All day long
You punch the doors of death to wake
A slain generation. Let them lie

Still. Let them sleep on,
O guns. Shake no more
(But leave the locks secure)
Hell's door.

SPRING STORM

When in their ignorance and haste the skies must fall
Upon our white-eyed home, and blindly turn
Feeling the four long limits of the wall,

How unsubstantial is our present state
In the clean blowing of those elements
Whose study is our problem and our fate?

The intellects go mumbling in the snow,
And find the blurred, incredible sun (and moon)
Jammed in the white door, and the troubled straits
The dugout where the fallen sky lies down.
A mess of secret trumpets, with their weight
Of portents, veil the bluntness where we run.

How true a passion has this hour begun!
The sky melts on my patient animal
(My pointless self, the hunter of my home),
My breath burns in the open like a ton
In the blue waking of those elements
Whose study is our quibble and our doom.

O watch the woolen hundreds on the run!

LANDSCAPE

1

A Personage is seen
Leaning upon a cushion
Printed with cornflowers.

A Child appears
Holding up a pencil.

"This is a picture
(Says the Child to the Personage)
Of the vortex."

"Draw it your own way,"
Says the Personage.

(Music is heard
Pure in the island windows,
Sea-music on the Child's
Interminable shore, his coral home.)

Behind a blue mountain
Covered with chickenfoot trees,
The molten sun appears,
A heavy, painted flower.

A Personage is seen
Leaning upon the mountain
With the sun in one hand
And a pencil in the other.

"This is a picture
(Says the Personage to the Child)
Of the beginning of the world."

"Or of its end!" cries the Child
Hiding himself in the cushions.

2

A Woman appears
Leaning upon the Child's shoulder.
He looks up again.

"This is my Mother
(Says the Child to the Personage)
Older than the moon."

(Grecian horses are heard
Returning from the foam
Of the pure island's windows,
And the Child's horizons.)

"My Mother is a world
(Says the Child to the Personage)
Printed with gillyflowers."

"Paint her your own way"
(Says the Personage to the Child).
And, lifting up his pencil,
He crosses out the sun.

BIRDCAGE WALK

1

One royal afternoon
When I was young and easily surprised
By uncles coming from the park
At the command of nurses and of guards,

I wondered, over trees and ponds,
At the sorry, rude walls
And the white windows of the apartments.
"These," said my uncle, "are the tallest houses."

2

Yes, in the spring of my joy
When I was visibly affected by a gaitered bishop,
Large and unsteady in the flagged yard,
Guards, dogs and blackbirds fled on every hand.

"He is an old one," said uncle,
"The gaiters are real."

3

Rippled, fistfed windows of your
Dun high houses! Then
Come cages made of pretty willows
Where they put the palace girls!
Green ducks wade slowly from the marble water.
One swan reproves a saucy daughter.

I consider my own true pond,
Look for the beginning and the end.
I lead the bishop down lanes and islands.

4

Yes, in the windows of my first existence
Before my yawns became seasons,
When nurses and uncles were sure,
Chinese fowl fought the frosty water
Startled by this old pontifex.

"No bridge" (He smiled
Between the budding branches),
"No crossing to the cage
Of the paradise bird!"

Astounded by the sermons in the leaves
I cried, "No! No! The stars have higher houses!"

Kicking the robins and ganders
From the floor of his insular world
The magic bishop leaned his blessing on the children.

5

That was the bold day when
Moved by the unexpected summons
I opened all the palace aviaries
As by a king's representative
I was appointed fowler.

WISDOM

I studied it and it taught me nothing.
I learned it and soon forgot everything else:
Having forgotten, I was burdened with knowledge—
The insupportable knowledge of nothing.

How sweet my life would be, if I were wise!
Wisdom is well known
When it is no longer seen or thought of.
Only then is understanding bearable.

TO A SEVERE NUN

I know, Sister, that solitude
Will never dismay you. You have chosen
A path too steep for others to follow.
I take it you prefer to go without them.

You will not complain that others are fickle
When they abandon you, renouncing the contest.
After all, they have not understood
That love is a contest, and that the love you demand
Is a match, in which you overcome your friends
After a long agony.

Thus you have no visible companions. Yet, drive on,
Drive on: do not consider your despair! Imagine
    rather
That there are many saints around you in the same
    desperation,
Violent, without contact, without responsibility,
Except of course to their own just souls
And to the God Who cannot blame them.

You know where you are going. You alone
In the whole convent know what bitter comfort
Eludes the malcontents who travel this unusual desert,
Seeking the impossible, and not the Absolute—
Sustained always by the same hate.

Do not be disconcerted, Sister, if in spite of your effort
The impertinent truth shows up weakness at least in
    others
And distracts you with their suffering.
Do not be humbled if, for an instant,
Christ seems glad to suffer in another.

Forget this scandal. Do not look at them
Or you may lose your nerve, and come to admit
That violence is your evasion and that you,
You most of all, are weak.

"WHEN IN THE SOUL OF THE SERENE DISCIPLE . . ."

When in the soul of the serene disciple
With no more Fathers to imitate
Poverty is a success,
It is a small thing to say the roof is gone:
He has not even a house.

Stars, as well as friends,
Are angry with the noble ruin.
Saints depart in several directions.

Be still:
There is no longer any need of comment.
It was a lucky wind
That blew away his halo with his cares,
A lucky sea that drowned his reputation.

Here you will find
Neither a proverb nor a memorandum.
There are no ways,
No methods to admire
Where poverty is no achievement.
His God lives in his emptiness like an affliction.

What choice remains?
Well, to be ordinary is not a choice:
It is the usual freedom
Of men without visions.

A PRACTICAL PROGRAM FOR MONKS

1

Each one shall sit at table with his own cup and
    spoon, and with his own repentance. Each one's
    own business shall be his most important affair,
    and provide his own remedies.
They have neglected bowl and plate.
Have you a wooden fork?
Yes, each monk has a wooden fork as well as a potato.

2

Each one shall wipe away tears with his own saint,
    when three bells hold in store a hot afternoon.
    Each one is supposed to mind his own heart, with
    its conscience, night and morning.
Another turn on the wheel: ho hum! And observe the
    Abbot!
Time to go to bed in a straw blanket.

3

Plenty of bread for everyone between prayers and the
    psalter: will you recite another?
Merci, and *Miserere.*
Always mind both the clock and the Abbot until
    eternity.
Miserere.

4

Details of the Rule are all liquid and solid. What
    canon was the first to announce regimentation
    before us? Mind the step on the way down!

Yes, I dare say you are right, Father. I believe you; I
believe you.
I believe it is easier when they have ice water and even
a lemon.
Each one can sit at table with his own lemon, and
mind his conscience.

5
Can we agree that the part about the lemon is regu-
lar?
In any case, it is better to have sheep than peacocks,
and cows rather than a chained leopard says
Modest, in one of his proverbs.
The monastery, being owner of a communal row-
boat, is the antechamber of heaven.
Surely that ought to be enough.

6
Each one can have some rain after Vespers on a hot
afternoon, but *ne quid nimis,* or the purpose of
the Order will be forgotten.
We shall send you hyacinths and a sweet millennium.
Everything the monastery provides is very pleasant to
see and to sell for nothing.
What is baked smells fine. There is a sign of God on
every leaf that nobody sees in the garden. The
fruit trees are there on purpose, even when no
one is looking. Just put the apples in the basket.
In Kentucky there is also room for a little cheese.
Each one shall fold his own napkin, and neglect the
others.

7

Rain is always very silent in the night, under such
    gentle cathedrals.
Yes, I have taken care of the lamp. *Miserere.*
Have you a patron saint, and an angel?
Thank you. Even though the nights are never danger-
    ous, I have one of everything.

SONG: IN THE SHOWS OF THE ROUND OX

i
In the shows of the round Ox
(O pagan night)
They fought their lucky stars.

Light of a wicked sun
And flying cars.

In the shows of the brass barn
(O fatal sun)
They lost a morning's fortune.

ii
"There is no game like money"
(Cries the man with the hand)
"So sell your brother".

Light of a gambling clock
And trained symbols.
When they win, they drown.

"There is no game like homeward"
Cry the whirlwind trumpeters.

iii
To the shallow water
They are standing on
These waterwalkers owe
No genuine fortune.

Strong ones have their own
Problems and pardons
For the iron ox.

iv
Tell me the name of the brass horn
That makes all the money.
Tell me the day of the wargames
Where gold is won.
The winning day is the day
On my green paper.
The first-last dollar's number
Is my own name.

v
The brass fighting cocks
And bloodred winners
Ask no pardon
And present no problem.

(But there is no game like pardon).

vi
The fight is over. Eyes of the furious Ox
Are brass suns. There is no game like standing on the
    water:

But there is no winner.

Strong ones have their own
Mercies and questions
For brazen fortune.

AN ELEGY FOR FIVE OLD LADIES

(*Newton, Mass., April 20: Five women ranging in age from 80
to 96 drowned this afternoon when a driverless car rolled across a
rest home lawn and sank in Crystal Lake* . . . THE NEW YORK
TIMES)

Let us forget that it is spring and celebrate the rider-
    less will of five victims.
Old companions are sitting silent in the home. Five of
    their number have suddenly gone too far, as if
    waifs,

As if orphans were to swim without license. Their
ride was not lucky. It took them very far out of
bounds.

Mrs. Watson said she saw them all go at three forty
five. Their bell had rung too loud and too late.

It was a season when water is too cold for anyone, and
is especially icy for an old person.

The brazen sedan was not to be trusted. The wheels
went too well for one short and straight journey.
It was the last: the doors did not open.

Dimly and too late they saw themselves on a very
wicked lawn. May God have mercy on their recre-
ation!

Let us accordingly pay homage to five now legendary
persons, the very chaste daughters of one unlucky
ride.

Let the perversity of a machine become our common
study, while I name loudly five loyal spouses of
death!

THE MOSLEMS' ANGEL OF DEATH

(Algeria 1961)

Like a jeweled peacock he stirs all over
With fireflies. He takes his pleasure in
Lights.

He is a great honeycomb of shining bees
Knowing every dust with sugar in it.
He has a million fueled eyes.

With all his eyes he explores life.

The firefly city stirs all over with knowledge.
His high buildings see too many
Persons: he has found out
Their times and when their windows
Will go out.

He turns the city lights in his fingers like money.

No other angel knows this one's place,
No other sees his phoenix wings, or understands
That he is lord of Death.

(Death was once allowed
To yell at the sky:
"I am death!
I take friend from friend!
I am death!
I leave your room empty!")

O night, O High Towers! No man can ever
Escape you, O night!

He is a miser. His fingers find the money.
He puts the golden lights in his pocket.

There is one red coal left burning
Beneath the ashes of the great vision.
There is one blood-red eye left open
When the city is burnt out.

Azrael! Azrael!
See the end of trouble!

O SWEET IRRATIONAL WORSHIP

Wind and a bobwhite
And the afternoon sun.

By ceasing to question the sun
I have become light,

Bird and wind.

My leaves sing.

I am earth, earth

All these lighted things
Grow from my heart.

A tall, spare pine
Stands like the initial of my first
Name when I had one.

When I had a spirit,
When I was on fire
When this valley was
Made out of fresh air
You spoke my name
In naming Your silence:
O sweet, irrational worship!

I am earth, earth

My heart's love
Bursts with hay and flowers.
I am a lake of blue air
In which my own appointed place
Field and valley
Stand reflected.

I am earth, earth

Out of my grass heart
Rises the bobwhite.

Out of my nameless weeds
His foolish worship.

A PICTURE OF LEE YING

She wears old clothes she holds a borrowed handker-
chief and her sorrow shows us the papers have bad
news again today Lee Ying only 19 has to return to
China

Days on foot with little or no food the last six days
on water alone now she must turn back

Three hundred thousand like her must turn back to
China there is no room say the officials in Hong
Kong you must go back where you came from

Point of no return is the caption but this is meaning-
less she must return that is the story

She would not weep if she had reached a point of no
return what she wants is not to return

There is no place for her and no point for thousands
like her there is no point

Their flight from bad news to worse news has caused
alarm

Refugees suffer and authorities feel alarm the press
does not take sides

We know all about the sorrow of Lee Ying one glance
is enough we look at something else

She must go back where she came from no more need
be said

Whenever the authorities are alarmed everyone must
return to China

We too know all about sorrow we have seen it in the
movies

You have our sympathy Miss Lee Ying you must go
where we are sorry for your future

Too bad some people get all the rough breaks the au-
thorities regret

Refugees from China have caused alarm

When the authorities are alarmed what can you do

You can return to China

Their alarm is worse than your sorrow

Please do not look only at the dark side in private
life these are kind men

They are only obeying orders

Over there is Red China where you will remain in
future

There also the authorities are alarmed and they too
obey orders

Please do not look only at the dark side

All the newspapers in the free world explain why you return their readers understand how you feel

You have the sympathy of millions

As a tribute to your sorrow we resolve to spend more money on nuclear weapons there is always a bright side

If this were only a movie a boat would be available have you ever seen our movies they end happily

You would lean at the rail with "him" the sun would set on China kiss and fade

You would marry one of the kind authorities

In our movies there is no law higher than love in real life duty is higher

You would not want the authorities to neglect duty

How do you like the image of the free world sorry you cannot stay

This is the first and last time we will see you in our papers

When you are back home remember us we will be having a good time

GRACE'S HOUSE

On the summit: it stands on a fair summit
Prepared by winds: and solid smoke
Rolls from the chimney like a snow cloud.
Grace's house is secure.

No blade of grass is not counted,
No blade of grass forgotten on this hill.
Twelve flowers make a token garden.
There is no path to the summit—
No path drawn
To Grace's house.

All the curtains are arranged
Not for hiding but for seeing out.
In one window someone looks out and winks.
Two gnarled short
Fortified trees have knotholes
From which animals look out.
From behind a corner of Grace's house
Another creature peeks out.

Important: hidden in the foreground
Most carefully drawn
The dog smiles, his foreleg curled, his eye like an aster.
Nose and collar are made with great attention:
This dog is loved by Grace!

And there: the world!
Mailbox number 5

Is full of Valentines for Grace.
There is a name on the box, name of a family
Not yet ready to be written in language.

A spangled arrow there
Points from our Coney Island
To her green sun-hill.

Between our world and hers
Runs a sweet river:
(No, it is not the road,
It is the uncrossed crystal
Water between our ignorance and her truth.)

O paradise, O child's world!
Where all the grass lives
And all the animals are aware!
The huge sun, bigger than the house
Stands and streams with life in the east
While in the west a thunder cloud
Moves away forever.

No blade of grass is not blessed
On this archetypal hill,
This womb of mysteries.

I must not omit to mention a rabbit
And two birds, bathing in the stream
Which is no road, because

Alas, there is no road to Grace's house!

III

LOVE WINTER WHEN THE PLANT SAYS NOTHING

O little forests, meekly
Touch the snow with low branches!
O covered stones
Hide the house of growth!

Secret
Vegetal words,
Unlettered water,
Daily zero.

Pray undistracted
Curled tree
Carved in steel—
Buried zenith!

Fire, turn inward
To your weak fort,
To a burly infant spot,
A house of nothing.

O peace, bless this mad place:
Silence, love this growth.

O silence, golden zero
Unsetting sun

Love winter when the plant says nothing.

WHAT TO THINK WHEN IT
RAINS BLOOD

(After a letter of Fulbert of Chartres to King Robert,—XI Cent.)

I have been instructed by your sacred Majesty to ex-
amine the histories, and see if a rain of blood is
recorded, and to tell your Majesty what such rain
portends.

I have found Livy, Valerius, Orosius and several others
who relate a portent of this kind. But for the present
let it suffice to summon one of them only as witness,
Gregory, Bishop of Tours, because of the authority of
his religious life.

This same Gregory declares, in the VI book of his
histories, and the IV chapter: "In the seventh year of
King Childebert, which was also the twenty first of
Childeric and Guntran, in the middle of winter there
was a summer downpour with lightning and frightful
thunder.

Blossoms flowered on the trees. That star which I have
before named 'comet' appeared again, having all
around itself an inky darkness, so that the comet ap-
peared to be looking out of a hole, glittering amid the
shadows and shaking its long hair.

Then there went forth from it a ray of awful magniture
which from afar looked like the smoke of a great fire.
This was seen in the western sky in the first hour of
the night.

Now on the holy day of Easter, in the city of Soissons, the sky was seen to burn, so that there appeared to be two conflagrations, the one greater and the other less. After the space of two hours these were joined together in one, and having been made into a huge signal-light, disappeared.

Then in the region of Paris true blood rained from a cloud and fell upon the garments of many persons, so soiling them that, stricken with horror at their own clothes, they tore them off and threw them away. And at three places within the city this prodigy appeared.

In the territory of Senlis, the house of a certain man, when he got up in the morning, was seen to be spattered all over, inside, with blood. And that year there was a great plague among the people.

Various illnesses, a honey-colored sickness, and also pustules and tumors caused the death of many. But others, who took care, lived.

We have also learned that in that year, in the city of Narbonne, a disease of the private parts raged so furiously that a man knew he was finished as soon as this punishment came upon him." Thus far Gregory of Tours.

It is evident therefore, from this and from the other histories I have mentioned, that a rain of blood foretells that thousands must soon perish in a great disaster.

Now if you have lately heard of this kind of rain falling upon a certain part of your kingdom,
And if you have learned that this blood-rain, falling on stone or on man's flesh, could not be washed away, Yet falling on wood could be washed away with ease: this seems to me to indicate three types of men.
The stones are impious men. Flesh represents fornicators. Wood, which is neither hard like stone nor soft like flesh, indicates those who are neither impious nor fornicators.

And therefore, when there shall descend upon those two kinds of men for whom it is predicted the sword of pestilence, designated by this rain of blood which sticks to them,
If they should be converted they will not be damned, dying for eternity in their blood.

As for those others to whom the blood-rain does not stick, they may well be set altogether free from their bondage by the anguish of death, or by some other means, according to the decision of the most secret and supreme Judge.

Farewell, religious King!

AND THE CHILDREN OF BIRMINGHAM

And the children of Birmingham
Walked into the story
Of Grandma's pointed teeth
("Better to love you with")
Reasonable citizens
Rose to exhort them all:
"Return at once to schools of friendship.
Buy in stores of love and law."
(And tales were told
Of man's best friend, the Law.)

And the children of Birmingham
Walked in the shadow
Of Grandma's devil
Smack up against
The singing wall.
Fire and water
Poured over everyone:
"Hymns were extreme,
So there could be no pardon!"

And old Grandma
Began the lesson
Of everybody's skin,
Everybody's fun:
"Liberty may bite
An irresponsible race
Forever singing,"
Grandma said,

"Forever making love:
Look at all the children!"

(And tales were told
Of man's best friend, the Law.)

And the children of Birmingham
Walked into the fury
Of Grandma's hug:
Her friendly cells
("Better to love you with.")
Her friendly officers
And "dooms of love."

Laws had a very long day
And all were weary.

But what the children did that time
Gave their town
A name to be remembered!

(And tales were told
Of man's best friend, the Law.)

CHANT TO BE USED IN PROCESSIONS AROUND A SITE WITH FURNACES

How we made them sleep and purified them

How we perfectly cleaned up the people and worked a big heater

I was the commander I made improvements and installed a guaranteed system taking account of human weakness I purified and I remained decent

How I commanded

I made cleaning appointments and then I made the travellers sleep and after that I made soap

I was born into a Catholic family but as these people were not going to need a priest I did not become a priest I installed a perfectly good machine it gave satisfaction to many

When trains arrived the soiled passengers received appointments for fun in the bathroom they did not guess

It was a very big bathroom for two thousand people it awaited arrival and they arrived safely

There would be an orchestra of merry widows not all the time much art

If they arrived at all they would be given a greeting
card to send home taken care of with good jobs
wishing you would come to our joke

Another improvement I made was I built the cham-
bers for two thousand invitations at a time the naked
votaries were disinfected with Zyklon B

Children of tender age were always invited by reason
of their youth they were unable to work they were
marked out for play

They were washed like the others and more than the
others

Very frequently women would hide their children in
the piles of clothing but of course when we came to
find them we would send the children into the cham-
ber to be bathed

How often I commanded and made improvements
and sealed the door on top there were flowers the
men came with crystals I guaranteed the crystal parlor

I guaranteed the chamber and it was sealed you could
see through portholes

They waited for the shower it was not hot water that
came through vents though efficient winds gave full
satisfaction portholes showed this

The satisfied all ran together to the doors awaiting
arrival it was guaranteed they made ends meet

How could I tell by their cries that love came to a
full stop I found the ones I had made clean after
about a half hour

Jewish male inmates then worked up nice they had
rubber boots in return for adequate food I could not
guess their appetite

Those at the door were taken apart out of a fully
stopped love by rubber male inmates strategic hair
and teeth being used later for defense

Then the males removed all clean love rings and made
away with happy gold

How I commanded and made soap 12 lbs fat 10
quarts water 8 oz to a lb of caustic soda but it was
hard to find any fat

A big new firm promoted steel forks operating on a
cylinder they got the contract and with faultless work-
manship delivered very fast goods

"For transporting the customers we suggest using
light carts on wheels a drawing is submitted"

"We acknowledge four steady furnaces and an emer-
gency guarantee"

"I am a big new commander operating on a cylinder
I elevate the purified materials boil for 2 to 3 hours
and then cool"

For putting them into a test fragrance I suggested an
express elevator operated by the latest cylinder it was
guaranteed

Their love was fully stopped by our perfected ovens
but the love rings were salvaged

Thanks to the satisfaction of male inmates operating
the heaters without need of compensation our guests
were warmed

All the while I had obeyed perfectly

So I was hanged in a commanding position with a
full view of the site plant and grounds

You smile at my career but you would do as I did if
you knew yourself and dared

In my day we worked hard we saw what we did our
self-sacrifice was conscientious and complete our work
was faultless and detailed

Do not think yourself better because you burn up
friends and enemies with long-range missiles without
ever seeing what you have done.

AN ELEGY FOR ERNEST HEMINGWAY

Now for the first time on the night of your death your name is mentioned in convents, *ne cadas in obscurum.*

Now with a true bell your story becomes final. Now men in monasteries, men of requiems, familiar with the dead, include you in their offices.

You stand anonymous among thousands, waiting in the dark at great stations on the edge of countries known to prayer alone, where fires are not merciless, we hope, and not without end.

You pass briefly through our midst. Your books and writings have not been consulted. Our prayers are *pro defuncto N.*

Yet some look up, as though among a crowd of prisoners or displaced persons, they recognized a friend once known in a far country. For these the sun also rose after a forgotten war upon an idiom you made great. They have not forgotten you. In their silence you are still famous, no ritual shade.

How slowly this bell tolls in a monastery tower for a whole age, and for the quick death of an unready dynasty, and for that brave illusion: the adventurous self!

For with one shot the whole hunt is ended!

ADVICE TO A YOUNG PROPHET

Keep away, son, these lakes are salt. These flowers
Eat insects. Here private lunatics
Yell and skip in a very dry country.

Or where some haywire monument
Some badfaced daddy of fear
Commands an unintelligent rite.

To dance on the unlucky mountain,
To dance they go, and shake the sin
Out of their feet and hands,

Frenzied until the sudden night
Falls very quiet, and magic sin
Creeps, secret, back again.

Badlands echo with omens of ruin:
Seven are very satisfied, regaining possession:
(Bring a little mescaline, you'll get along!)

There's something in your bones,
There's someone dirty in your critical skin,
There's a tradition in your cruel misdirected finger
Which you must obey, and scribble in the hot sand:

"Let everybody come and attend
Where lights and airs are fixed
To teach and entertain. O watch the sandy people
Hopping in the naked bull's-eye,

Shake the wildness out of their limbs,
Try to make peace like John in skins
Elijah in the timid air
or Anthony in tombs:

Pluck the imaginary trigger, brothers.
Shoot the devil: he'll be back again!"

America needs these fatal friends
Of God and country, to grovel in mystical ashes,
Pretty big prophets whose words don't burn,
Fighting the strenuous imago all day long.

Only these lunatics (O happy chance)
Only these are sent. Only this anaemic thunder
Grumbles on the salt flats, in rainless night:

O go home, brother, go home!
The devil's back again,
And magic Hell is swallowing flies.

THE FALL

There is no where in you a paradise that is no place
    and there
You do not enter except without a story.

To enter there is to become unnameable.

Whoever is there is homeless for he has no door and
    no identity with which to go out and to come in.

Whoever is nowhere is nobody, and therefore cannot
    exist except as unborn:
No disguise will avail him anything

Such a one is neither lost nor found.

But he who has an address is lost.

They fall, they fall into apartments and are securely
    established!

They find themselves in streets. They are licensed
To proceed from place to place
They now know their own names
They can name several friends and know
Their own telephones must some time ring.

If all telephones ring at once, if all names are shouted
    at once and all cars crash at one crossing:
If all cities explode and fly away in dust

Yet identities refuse to be lost. There is a name and
number for everyone.

There is a definite place for bodies, there are pigeon
holes for ashes:
Such security can business buy!

Who would dare to go nameless in so secure a uni-
verse?
Yet, to tell the truth, only the nameless are at home
in it.

They bear with them in the center of nowhere the
unborn flower of nothing:
This is the paradise tree. It must remain unseen until
words end and arguments are silent.

NIGHT-FLOWERING CACTUS

I know my time, which is obscure, silent and brief
For I am present without warning one night only.

When sun rises on the brass valleys I become serpent.

Though I show my true self only in the dark and to
no man
(For I appear by day as serpent)
I belong neither to night nor day.

Sun and city never see my deep white bell
Or know my timeless moment of void:
There is no reply to my munificence.

When I come I lift my sudden Eucharist
Out of the earth's unfathomable joy
Clean and total I obey the world's body
I am intricate and whole, not art but wrought passion
Excellent deep pleasure of essential waters
Holiness of form and mineral mirth:

I am the extreme purity of virginal thirst.

I neither show my truth nor conceal it
My innocence is described dimly
Only by divine gift
As a white cavern without explanation.

He who sees my purity
Dares not speak of it.
When I open once for all my impeccable bell
No one questions my silence:
The all-knowing bird of night flies out of my mouth.

Have you seen it? Then though my mirth has
    quickly ended
You live forever in its echo:
You will never be the same again.

WHY SOME LOOK UP TO PLANETS AND HEROES

Brooding and seated at the summit
Of a well-engineered explosion
He prepared his thoughts for fireflies and warnings

Only a tourist only a shy American
Flung into public sky by an ingenious weapon
Prepared for every legend

His space once visited by apes and Russians
No longer perfectly pure
Still proffered virginal joys and free rides
In his barrel of fun
A starspangled somersault
A sky-high Mother's Day

Four times that day his sun would set
Upon the casual rider
Streaking past the stars
At seventeen thousand miles per hour

Our winning Rover delighted
To remain hung up in cool hours and long trips
Smiling and riding in eternal transports

Even where a dog died in a globe
And still comes round enclosed
In a heaven of Russian wires

Uncle stayed alive
Gone in a globe of light
Ripping around the pretty world of girls and sights

"It will be fun" he thinks
"If by my cunning flight
The ignorant and Africans become convinced"

Convinced of what? Nobody knows
And Major is far out
Four days ahead of his own news

Until at last the shy American smiles
Colliding once again with air fire and lenses
To stand on noisy earth
And engineer consent

Consent to what? Nobody knows
What engine next will dig a moon
What costly uncles stand on Mars

What next device will fill the air with burning dollars
Or else lay out the low down number of some Day
What day? May we consent?
Consent to what? Nobody knows.
Yet the computers are convinced
Fed full of numbers by the True Believers.

THERE HAS TO BE A JAIL FOR LADIES

There has to be a jail where ladies go
When they are poor, without nice things, and with
    their hair down.
When their beauty is taken from them, when their
    hearts are broken
There is a jail where they must go.

There has to be a jail for ladies, says the Government,
When they are ugly because they are wrong.
It is good for them to stay there a long time
Until the wrong is forgotten.

When no one wants to kiss them any more,
Or only wants to kiss them for money
And take their beauty away
It is right for the wrong to be unheard of for a long
    time
Until the ladies are not remembered.

But I remember one favorite song,
And you ladies may not have forgotten:
"Poor broken blossom, poor faded flower," says my
    song.

Poor ladies, you are jailed roses:
When you speak you curse, when you curse
God and Hell are rusted together in one red voice
Coming as sweet as dust out of a little hollow heart.
Is there no child, then, in that empty heart?

Poor ladies, if you ever sang
It would be brown notes and sad, from understand-
    ing too much
No amount of soapsy sudsy supersuds will make you
Dainty again and not guilty
Until the very end, when you are all forgotten.
There is a jail, where guilt is not forgotten.

Not many days, or many years of that stale wall, that
    smell of disinfectant
Trying, without wanting, to kill your sin
Can make you innocent again:
So I come with this sad song
I love you, dusty and sore,
I love you, unhappy ones.

You are jailed buttercups, you are small field flowers,
To me your voice is not brown
Nor is God rusted together with Hell.
Tell me, darlings, can God be in Hell?
You may curse; but He makes your dry voice turn to
    butter
(Though for the policeman it is still brown)
God becomes your heart's prisoner, He will laugh at
    judges.
He will laugh at the jail.
He will make me write this song.

Keep me in your pocket if you have one. Keep me in
    your heart if you have no pocket.

It is not right for your sorrow to be unknown for-
    ever.
Therefore I come with these voices:

Poor ladies, do not despair—
God will come to your window with skylarks
And pluck each year like a white rose.

ELEGY FOR JAMES THURBER

Thurber, they have come, the secret bearers,
At the right time, though fools seem to have won.
Business and generals survive you
At least for one brief day.

Humor is now totally abolished.
The great dogs of nineteen sixty-one
Are nothing to laugh at.

Leave us, good friend. Leave our awful celebration
With pity and relief.
You are not called to solemnize with us
Our final madness.

You have not been invited to hear
The last words of everybody.

A MESSENGER FROM THE HORIZON

Look, a naked runner
A messenger,
Following the wind
From budding hills.

By sweet sunstroke
Wounded and signed,
(He is therefore sacred)
Silence is his way.

Rain is his own
Most private weather.
Amazement is his star.

O stranger, our early hope
Flies fast by,
A mute comet, an empty sun.
Adam is his name!

O primeval angel
Virgin brother of astonishment,
Born of one word, one bare
Inquisitive diamond.

O blessed,
Invulnerable cry,
O unplanned Saturday,
O lucky father!

Come without warning
A friend of hurricanes,
Lightning in your bones!
We will open to you
The sun-door, the noble eye!

Open to rain, to somersaulting air,
To everything that swims,
To skies that wake,
Flare and applaud.

(It is too late, he flies the other way
Wrapping his honesty in rain.)

*　　*　　*

Pardon all runners,
All speechless, alien winds,
All mad waters.

Pardon their impulses,
Their wild attitudes,
Their young flights, their reticence.

When a message has no clothes on
How can it be spoken?

SONG FOR NOBODY

A yellow flower
(Light and spirit)
Sings by itself
For nobody.

A golden spirit
(Light and emptiness)
Sings without a word
By itself.

Let no one touch this gentle sun
In whose dark eye
Someone is awake.

(No light, no gold, no name, no color
And no thought:
O, wide awake!)

A golden heaven
Sings by itself
A song to nobody.

INDEX OF FIRST LINES

Complete descriptive catalog available free on request from
New Directions, 333 Sixth Avenue, New York 10014.   † Bilingual